UNDERSTANDING LANGUAGE TEACHING: REASONING IN ACTION

Karen E. Johnson

The Pennsylvania State University

A TeacherSource Book

Donald Freeman
Series Editor

Australia • Brazil • Japan • Korea • Mexico • Singapore • Spain • United Kingdom • United States

**Understanding Language Teaching:
Reasoning in Action**
Karen E. Johnson

Editorial Director: Erik Gundersen

Marketing Director: Charlotte Sturdy

Production Services Coordinator: Mike
　Burggren

Developmental Editor: Thomas Healy

Vice President and Publisher/ESL: Stanley
　J. Galek

Designer: Jessica Robison

Production: Su Wilson

Project Management and Composition:
　Imageset

Manufacturing Coordinator: Mary Beth
　Hennebury

Associate Market Development Director:
　Mary Sutton

Cover Designer: Ha D. Nguyen

For product information and technology assistance, contact us at
Cengage Learning Customer & Sales Support, 1-800-354-9706

For permission to use material from this text or product,
submit all requests online at **cengage.com/permissions**
Further permissions questions can be emailed to
permissionrequest@cengage.com

ISBN-13: 978-0-8384-6690-2

ISBN-10: 0-8384-6690-7

Heinle
25 Thomson Place
Boston, MA 02210
USA

Cengage Learning is a leading provider of customized learning solutions with office locations around the globe, including Singapore, the United Kingdom, Australia, Mexico, Brazil, and Japan. Locate your local office at:
international.cengage.com/region

Cengage Learning products are represented in Canada by
Nelson Education, Ltd.

For your course and learning solutions, visit **academic.cengage.com**

Purchase any of our products at your local college store or at our preferred online store **www.ichapters.com**

Printed in the United States of America
5 6 7 8 9　　　20 19 18 17 16

TABLE OF CONTENTS

Thank You

The series editor, authors and publisher would like to thank the following individuals who offered many helpful insights throughout the development of the TeacherSource series.

Jo Ann Aebersold	Eastern Michigan University
Linda Lonon Blanton	University of New Orleans
Tommie Brasel	New Mexico School for the Deaf
Jill Burton	University of South Australia
Margaret B. Cassidy	Brattleboro Union High School, Vermont
Florence Decker	University of Texas at El Paso
Silvia G. Diaz	Dade County Public Schools, Florida
Margo Downey	Boston University
David E. Eskey	University of Southern California
Alvino Fantini	School for International Training
Sandra Fradd	University of Miami
Jerry Gebhard	Indiana University of Pennsylvania
Fred Genesee	University of California at Davis
Stacy Gildenston	Colorado State University
Jeannette Gordon	Illinois Resource Center
Else Hamayan	Illinois Resource Center
Sarah Hudelson	Arizona State University
Joan Jamieson	Northern Arizona University
Elliot L. Judd	University of Illinois at Chicago
Donald N. Larson	Bethel College, Minnesota (Emeritus)
Numa Markee	University of Illinois at Urbana Champaign
Denise E. Murray	San Jose State University
Meredith Pike-Baky	University of California at Berkeley
Sara L. Sanders	Coastal Carolina University
Lilia Savova	Indiana University of Pennsylvania
Donna Sievers	Garden Grove Unified School District, California
Ruth Spack	Tufts University
Leo van Lier	Monterey Institute of International Studies

To Glenn & Elizabeth

ACKNOWLEDGMENTS

This book was a blast to write. In part, it may have been because I was on sabbatical and I actually had time to think and write; a true luxury in today's professional world. For this, I thank my colleague, Dennis Gouran, for somehow making it possible for me to be on leave at a time when it seemed absolutely impossible for me to do so.

I also enjoyed writing this book because it is about something for which I care deeply; language teachers and language teaching. For this, I wish to thank the many teachers with whom I have worked over the years. If it had not been for their willingness to open up their minds, lives, and classrooms to me, the ideas that have evolved in me and are now part of this book would never have come to fruition. In particular, I wish to thank Ken Pransky, Anne Campbell, and Elizabeth Morrison for welcoming me and the entire language teaching profession into their classrooms. Their stories and teaching will change the way teachers think about language teaching forever.

But probably the main reason why this book was so much fun to write was because I finally had a chance to say what I think is important about teacher learning and professional development in language teacher education. For this, I am indebted to my friend and colleague, Donald Freeman, for coming up with the **TeacherSource** concept, making sure it became a reality and, more personally, for his keen insights into my work, which always push me beyond my current thinking and make my rethinking and rewriting process a true learning experience.

And finally, I thank my best friend and husband, Glenn, for his infinite patience, unwavering support, and enduring love.

SERIES EDITOR'S PREFACE

As I was driving just south of White River Junction, the snow had started falling in earnest. The light was flat, although it was mid-morning, making it almost impossible to distinguish the highway in the gray-white swirling snow. I turned on the radio, partly as a distraction and partly to help me concentrate on the road ahead; the announcer was talking about the snow. "The state highway department advises motorists to use extreme caution and to drive with their headlights on to ensure maximum visibility." He went on, his tone shifting slightly, "Ray Burke, the state highway supervisor, just called to say that one of the plows almost hit a car just south of Exit 6 because the person driving hadn't turned on his lights. He really wants people to put their headlights on because it is very tough to see in this stuff." I checked, almost reflexively, to be sure that my headlights were on, as I drove into the churning snow.

How can information serve those who hear or read it in making sense of their own worlds? How can it enable them to reason about what they do and to take appropriate actions based on that reasoning? My experience with the radio in the snow storm illustrates two different ways of providing the same message: the need to use your headlights when you drive in heavy snow. The first offers dispassionate information; the second tells the same content in a personal, compelling story. The first disguises its point of view; the second explicitly grounds the general information in a particular time and place. Each means of giving information has its role, but I believe the second is ultimately more useful in helping people make sense of what they are doing. When I heard Ray Burke's story about the plow, I made sure my headlights were on.

In what is written about teaching, it is rare to find accounts in which the author's experience and point of view are central. A point of view is not simply an opinion; neither is it a whimsical or impressionistic claim. Rather, a point of view lays out what the author thinks and why; to borrow the phrase from writing teacher Natalie Goldberg, "it sets down the bones." The problem is that much of what is available in professional development in language-teacher education concentrates on telling rather than on point of view. The telling is prescriptive, like the radio announcer's first statement. It emphasizes what is important to know and do, what is current in theory and research, and therefore what you—as a practicing teacher—should do. But this telling disguises the teller; it hides the point of view that can enable you to make sense of what is told.

The **TeacherSource** series offers you a point of view on second/foreign language teaching. Each author in this series has had to lay out what she or he believes is central to the topic, and how she or he has come to this understanding. So as a reader, you will find this book has a personality; it is not anonymous. It comes as a story, not as a directive, and it is meant to create a relationship with you rather than assume your attention. As a practitioner, its point of view can help you in your own work by providing a sounding board for your ideas and a metric for your own thinking. It can suggest courses of action and explain why these make sense to the author. And you can take from it what you will, and do with it what you can. This book will not tell you what to think; it is meant to help you make sense of what you do.

The point of view in **TeacherSource** is built out of three strands: **Teachers' Voices**, **Frameworks**, and **Investigations.** Each author draws together these strands uniquely, as suits his or her topic and more crucially his or her point of view. All materials in **TeacherSource** have these three strands. The **Teachers' Voices** are practicing language teachers from various settings who tell about their experience of the topic. The **Frameworks** lay out what the author believes is important to know about his or her topic and its key concepts and issues. These fundamentals define the area of language teaching and learning about which she or he is writing. The **Investigations** are meant to engage you, the reader, in relating the topic to your own teaching, students, and classroom. They are activities which you can do alone or with colleagues, to reflect on teaching and learning and/or try out ideas in practice.

Each strand offers a point of view on the book's topic. The **Teachers' Voices** relate the points of view of various practitioners; the **Frameworks** establish the point of view of the professional community; and the **Investigations** invite you to develop your own point of view, through experience with reference to your setting. Together these strands should serve in making sense of the topic.

Karen Johnson's work has been at the heart of **TeacherSource** since its inception. She and her husband, Glenn Johnson, first developed the CD-ROM version of *Teachers Understanding Teaching* in which they created a multimedia environment to capture the essential dynamic processes of sense-making. Users of this program actively construct their individual paths, which lead to understanding their own teaching through interaction and dialogue with three teachers, Ken, Elizabeth, and Anne. In this book, Karen Johnson carries forward these same ideas to examine closely how teachers learn their craft. She has been a central thinker in the development of teacher cognition in the field of language teaching. In *Understanding Language Teaching: Reasoning in Action* you will find Johnson is more explicit about her point of view. She argues that learning to teach involves developing "robust reasoning" and that by understanding their own thinking, teachers can truly possess and direct their work. This book and the accompanying CD-ROM can prove invaluable tools for teachers who seek to better understand what they do in their classrooms and why.

This book, like all elements of the **TeacherSource** series, is intended to serve you in understanding your work as a language teacher. It may lead you to thinking about what you do in different ways and/or to taking specific actions in your teaching. Or it may do neither. But we intend, through the variety of points of view presented in this fashion, to offer you access to choices in teaching that you may not have thought of before and thus to help your teaching make more sense.

— *Donald Freeman, Series Editor*

Author's Preface

For the past 10 years I have worked as a teacher educator in a graduate-level master's in TESOL program at a large North American university. Each semester I supervise the teaching experiences of at least ten and sometimes as many as twenty pre-service and in-service ESL and EFL teachers. Some of these teachers are new to teaching; others come with many years of teaching experience. Most are female, some are male. Most are in their mid-twenties or early thirties; some are older. Some are American and want to teach ESL in America, while others want to live and travel while teaching EFL abroad. Still others are natives of countries and cultures from around the globe, and fully expect to return to those lands to teach EFL. Almost all of them have lived, worked, or traveled in other countries and speak a second or even a third language. And while the particulars of their living, learning, and teaching experiences certainly differ, I always find that the ways they all think about teaching seem to be much more similar than different. It is the thinking about, or the reasoning, that is the focus of this book.

Most of the teachers who share their voices in this book spent time with me in my master's in TESOL program. Those who did not are experienced ESL teachers from elementary, secondary, or intensive English programs who participated in an instructional research project that formed the basis of the *Teachers Understanding Teaching* multimedia CD-ROM program, also published in the **TeacherSource** series (see below). So while the teachers featured in this book may come from the North American ESL instructional context, I believe their stories, their teaching, and their reasoning will seem remarkably similar to your own.

Since the focus of this book is on the reasoning that shapes the doing of teaching, the intended audience for this book is teachers who are actually teaching, in either a practicum or in-service setting. The Teachers' Voices and Frameworks sections of this book are certainly relevant for all readers. If you are currently teaching, the Investigations will enable you to develop a fuller understanding of your own reasoning and your own teaching. If you are not now teaching, you may want to arrange access to real classrooms, students, and/or teachers in order to carry out some of the Investigations. As with any learning opportunity, the more time and energy you put into the reading and doing of this book, the more you will gain from your experiences here.

Throughout this book, this CD-ROM icon is used to cross-reference Investigations that can also be found in the *Teachers Understanding Teaching* (Johnson & Johnson, 1998) multimedia hypertext tool. Part of the **TeacherSource** series, *Teachers Understanding Teaching* is an interactive CD-ROM software program designed to enable both novice and experienced ESL and EFL teachers to think critically both about themselves as teachers and about their own teaching. Constructed in a multimedia hypertext environment, the program allows teachers to create a highly individualized, self-directed learning environment where they can come to understand the interrelationships between what they know, believe, and think about second language teaching and learning and what they do in their classrooms.

The program is based on the professional experiences of three ESL teachers, Ken, Anne, and Elizabeth, at the elementary, secondary, and pre-university levels, as they reason in action. These three teachers are featured in Chapters 6, 7, and 8 of this book. In the CD-ROM program, their teaching practices are organized and accessed based on their instructional considerations, whereas in this book, they are presented as whole lessons, laid out from beginning to end, based on transcripts of their actual teaching practices and reflective comments about their teaching practices, and understood through the reasoning they engage in as they teach.

If you are already familiar with the *Teachers Understanding Teaching* program, you may find it helpful to view the reasoning of each of these teachers within the context of one entire lesson as presented in this book. If you are not familiar with *Teachers Understanding Teaching* you may find that program useful as a way to explore the lives and reasoning of these three teachers in more depth than is available in this book. In contrast, this book includes Teachers' Voices, Frameworks, and Investigations that are not in the CD-ROM program. Both the book and the CD-ROM program will supplement any professional development activities you are engaged in, enabling you to think critically about yourself as a teacher, your own reasoning, and your own teaching practices.

1
REASONING TEACHING

IT DEPENDS

Most of the teachers with whom I work jokingly complain that my standard answer to any question they have about teaching is "It depends." They ask, "Should we teach grammar rules explicitly?" and I respond, "It depends. Who are your students and what do you expect them to be able to do with explicit knowledge of grammar rules?" They ask, "Should we cover all the material in the chapter?" and I respond, "It depends. Do your students need to know all this material; what do they already know; and what else might they need to know that is not included in the chapter?"

I am not trying to engage my teachers in Rogerian psychotherapy—in my mind, it really does depend. I believe there is no one right way to teach and there are no simple answers to the complexities of teaching. Knowing what to do in any classroom depends on who your students are, what they know, and what they need to know. It depends on who you are, what you know and believe, and what you want your students to be able to know and do. It depends on what you are expected to teach, how you teach it, and what your students are expected to do with what you have taught them. It depends on how your students view you and to what extent they value what you are trying to teach them. It depends on how your students are viewed within the school where you teach and within the community where your school is located.

The list goes on and on. Knowing what to do in any classroom depends on a wide range of considerations, and the ways in which teachers think about these considerations, or what I have come to call **reasoning teaching,** lie at the core of both learning to teach and understanding teaching.

I see reasoning teaching as representing the cognitive activity that undergirds teachers' practices: the reasoning that determines the doing of teaching. I use the term "reasoning" rather than "thinking" as a way to expand the traditional notion of "teacher thinking" (see Clark & Peterson, 1986; Shavelson, 1983) from one that describes *what* teachers think about before, during, and after they teach, to one that includes *how* teachers think about these things within the context of their own classrooms. Thus, reasoning teaching represents the complex ways in which teachers conceptualize, construct explanations for, and respond to the social interactions and shared meanings that exist within and among teachers, students, parents, and administrators, both inside and outside the classroom. Simply put, reasoning teaching reflects the complex ways in which teachers figure out how to teach a particular topic, with a particular group of students, at a particular time, in a particular classroom, within a particular school.

I believe teachers' reasoning is grounded in teachers' knowledge and beliefs; that is, what they know and believe about teachers and teaching, where their knowledge and beliefs come from, their particular views of students and learning, and how they make sense of their own teaching. I believe teachers' reasoning occurs in and is shaped by the places where those teachers work; making all of teaching local and dependent on particular circumstances in specific classrooms with particular students. By coming to understand teaching through teachers' reasoning we are able to recognize and appreciate the ways in which teachers' accumulation of knowledge and beliefs based on their own learning and teaching experiences construct the interpretive frameworks through which they make sense of themselves as teachers, of their own teaching practices, and of the classrooms and schools where they work. Moreover, we are able to capture the highly situated, interpretive, and at times idiosyncratic qualities of real teaching—the messiness that is inherent in the ways in which teachers think about what they do.

While all teachers engage in reasoning, the robustness of such reasoning varies greatly among teachers, and not necessarily along the traditional lines of novice versus experienced teachers. By robustness I mean the completeness of their understandings of themselves, their students, and the classrooms and schools where they work, the flexibility with which they make use of these understandings, the complexity of their reasoning, and the range of instructional considerations they use as they carry out their professional activities.

In one sense, robust reasoning may seem similar to Prabhu's notion of "teachers' sense of plausibility," in other words, their "subjective understandings of the teaching they do" (1990, p. 172). Prabhu argues that teachers' sense of plausibility must be engaged if even the "best" of teaching practices are to avoid the natural tendency of becoming overroutinized and mechanical. However, robust reasoning is much more than maintaining an active sense of plausibility that is "alive, open to change, and more 'real' than mechanical" (1990, p. 173). Robust reasoning emerges when teachers expand their understandings of themselves, their teaching, their students, and their classrooms and schools. It emerges when teachers engage in a continual process of "criss-crossing" their professional landscape, seeing and experiencing it from multiple perspectives, recognizing its inherent complexity, and considering the interconnectedness of its various components. Robust reasoning occurs when teachers are able to assemble and apply their knowledge of their professional landscape flexibly so that it can be used in different situations and for different purposes (see Spiro et al., 1987).

This is why, as a teacher educator, I respond to my teachers' queries with, "It depends." Asking teachers to think about teaching in this way supports the kind of reasoning that will enable them not only to recognize that it depends, but to articulate what it depends on, enabling them to expand their knowledge of their professional landscapes and use that knowledge flexibly in different contexts and for different purposes and, in turn, offer both "real" (Prabhu, 1990) and effective classroom practice.

My goal in writing this book is to create multiple opportunities for teachers to understand the practice of teaching through the reasoning that determines that practice. Therefore, throughout this book you will have opportunities to both engage in and reflect on the reasoning that determines your practice and the practices of other teachers. You will have opportunities to examine the ways in which teachers think about themselves, their students, their teaching, and the social contexts in which they teach. You will have opportunities to explore the highly situated and interpretive nature of teachers' interactive decisions while they engage in real teaching in real classrooms. And you will have opportunities to investigate the ways in which teachers conceptualize and resolve the problems and dilemmas they face in the places where they work.

Such opportunities, I believe, will enable you to understand teaching in its natural form; to examine the complexities that make teaching a highly situated and interpretive activity; to know that in teaching it always "depends"; to be able to articulate, to yourself and others, the full range of considerations that it depends on; and to develop robust reasoning that will continually inform and reform your teaching practices.

Our journey begins (and will end—see Chapter 9) with a conversation I had with a teacher I supervised during her two-year master's in TESOL program at my university. Through our conversation, we catch glimpses of her reasoning—how she constructs an understanding of and an explanation for a particular lesson based on what she knows about herself, her students, and the instructional context in which she teaches. Exploring her reasoning in this way is essential if I, as her supervisor, am to truly understand her teaching, since I cannot presume to know why she teaches the way she does unless I understand the reasoning that undergirds her classroom practice. More important, I cannot attempt to alter her classroom practices unless I provide her with opportunities to modify and, in some cases, transform the nature of her reasoning.

Emily: Exploring the Landscape

Like most teachers who are teaching something new for the first time, Emily had lots of questions about the freshman composition course she was teaching for undergraduate ESL students. With an undergraduate degree in elementary education and two years of EFL teaching experience abroad, Emily was relatively confident in her abilities as a teacher but less so in her ability to teach academic writing at the university level. As a graduate student in our program, Emily was offered a teaching assistantship while completing her master's degree in TESOL. In addition to the formal training program that all teaching assistants participate in as part of the master's program, Emily often dropped by my office to talk informally about her teaching. One of our earlier conversations took the following path.

Emily: I was wondering if we could talk about my lesson for next week?

Karen: Sure, what do you have in mind?

Emily: Well, I'm not really sure. The book lists all these different ways of prewriting; cubing, linking, webbing . . . there are lots of examples, but I'm not really sure what to do with them. I mean, I guess we could do each one, but that seems pretty boring, and I don't know how useful these really are anyway. I certainly don't use any of these when I'm getting ready to write something, but I guess they'd be helpful if you didn't know where to begin . . .

Karen: What do you do when you're getting ready to write?

Emily: Me? Well, I do most of it in my head, I guess. I think about things when I'm in the shower, or whatever, and I don't actually start writing until I'm kind of sure of what I want to say. Of course, it always changes when I start writing, but once I sit down to write, I at least know where I'm going.

Karen: Do you think your students prewrite in their heads too?

Emily: I don't know. I suppose some do. I suppose I could ask them—that might be interesting. Do you think I should ask them what they do?

Karen: It depends. What would it tell you?

Emily: Well, at least I'd know where they were coming from, I'd be tapping into their prior knowledge [said authoritatively]. So I guess I could start with that. Yeah, I could ask them to talk about the ways they prewrite.

Karen: How will you do this?

Emily: How? Well, I could ask them.

Karen: What if they say they don't know?

Emily: Yeah, that's what usually happens when I ask things like that. . . . I guess they'd have to think about it for a while. I could ask them to think about the last paper they wrote and have them free-write about what they did when they started writing. This could be interesting. . . . I bet most of them don't even prewrite. I bet they'd tell me that too: "Like, why do we have to do all this prewriting stuff? Can't we just write?"

Karen: Is that OK?

Emily: Yeah, I guess so. I don't really, but the book has these strategies for prewriting that I'm supposed to cover. Do you think I even need to cover these?

Karen: It depends. Do you think they need to know how to use these strategies?

Emily: I don't know. Well, I guess if you really don't know what you want to write about they can help you think about the topic in a visual way and they can help you lay out what you already know about a topic. Some students might find them helpful, so I guess I should go over them, just so they know there are some strategies out there that can help them. Who knows, maybe if I used them [prewriting strategies] I wouldn't be such an anxious prewriter.

Karen: You're an anxious prewriter?

Emily: Yeah, I wander around for days trying to figure out what I want to say. I do things like clean my room before I start writing, but I'm usually thinking about it while I'm cleaning or whatever, and then when I finally sit down to write, I have some idea of what I want to say.

Karen: Do you think your students do this too?

Emily: I bet some of them do, so I guess I should spend some class time going over these strategies. But I want to make this fun; our last couple of classes were sort of boring. I don't know, they just weren't into it, sometimes the exercises in the book are pretty boring.

Karen: Well, what do you want them to get out of this lesson?

Emily: I want them to know there are some strategies they can use to get started but they shouldn't feel like they have to use them. I mean, everybody prewrites differently, right? And this whole process approach thing is supposed to be individual and cyclical, right? So, if they know of some other strategies that already work for them, they should know it's OK to use them. I just don't know how realistic it is to make them do all these fancy prewriting strategies given in the book. I mean, do I need to test them on this stuff?

Karen: It depends. If you did, what would it tell you?

Emily: Well, I don't know. I guess whether they can do them [prewriting strategies] or not, but not if they find them helpful as they start to write a paper and that's what's really important to me. I don't really care if they do cubing or not, I just want them to know there are strategies out there that they can use if they need help. So I guess I just want them to try a few of these, to get some hands-on experience with them, and then they can do whatever works for them.

Karen: So, is this the overall purpose of your lesson?

Emily: Well, I guess so, because I want them to think about the prewriting strategies they already use but I also want to offer them some other ways of prewriting that may be helpful. But I don't think each student needs to try every strategy; maybe they could each do one or two. Or maybe I could have different groups of students try out different strategies.

Karen: On the same topic?

Emily: Yeah, the groups could all work on the same topic but each group could use a different prewriting strategy. Then we could compare what they came up with: how was the cubing group's different from the webbing group's, and that way they wouldn't think that one strategy is better than another, or that they have to use all of them, but that different prewriting strategies might work for different writers. This could be sort of fun.

Karen: How so?

Emily: Well, they'd just be doing one strategy which wouldn't be so boring and I'll let them pick the topic or I could suggest one, 'cause last week I heard them talking about that straight group on campus —whatever they are calling themselves, you know, the ones who want official university recognition in the same way that the gay and lesbian groups do—they were arguing about it and some of the students didn't even see why it was an issue at all. I know this topic would get things rolling, they love to talk about these kinds of issues.

Our conversation highlights some of the considerations that shape Emily's reasoning. For Emily, her own experiences as a writer shape her conception of and the value she places on the set of prewriting activities outlined in her textbook. Her own experiences as a writer and those she suspects her students use shape her justification for teaching these prewriting activities in this particular manner. What she knows about her students' interests influences the topic she plans to suggest for small group discussion.

Clearly, Emily's reasoning is evolving. She seems concerned, as many teachers do, about covering all of the material in the textbook. She also seems to believe that the use of prewriting strategies is how writers should write, or that she might be a better writer if she used these strategies. Our conversation allowed Emily to explore her own personal views on prewriting strategies and to construct an explanation for how these strategies might be of value for her students. Our conversation created an opportunity for her to explore her personal beliefs about writing; contrast these beliefs with the possible needs of her students; articulate a goal and a plan for this lesson; and receive validation from a perceived authority, me, that her conception of and her approach toward this lesson were "OK."

What if I had indicated that I believe students need to master the intricacies of formulaic prewriting strategies and that she should test them on their ability to do so? How would this tidbit of information have shaped Emily's reasoning? By virtue of the status differential between us, Emily would probably have to reconceptualize her approach to this lesson. But would it have worked for her? I doubt it. Why? Because in Emily's mind, formulaic prewriting strategies have had little value to her as a writer, and she has no counterevidence to convince her otherwise. If, over time, she gains firsthand experience in her own writing—or even vicariously through her students' writing—that such strategies have more positive outcomes, she will probably reconceptualize her approach to this lesson. However, without critically reflecting on the way she has conceptualized this lesson and without exposure to alternative perspectives on the role of formulaic prewriting strategies in second language writing instruction, Emily will probably continue to base her reasoning on what she already knows; whether it be experiential knowledge as a writer, knowledge of her students, theoretical knowledge about how writers write, or pedagogical knowledge about how to teach second language writing. Moreover, the weighing of these types of knowledge will continue to vary as well. At this point in her professional development, Emily's firsthand experiences as a writer seem to weigh heavier than her secondhand theoretical knowledge about how writers write or her pedagogical knowledge about how to teach second language writing.

For Emily, and for all of the teachers with whom I work, it is essential to develop complex, flexible, conceptual understandings of the landscapes in which they work and to be able to use those understandings flexibly to carry out their teaching practices. And while *what* Emily and I talked about may be specific to her particular instructional context, *how* we talk about these things is much more ubiquitous to how all teachers reason. Exploring and expanding teachers' reasoning through reflection and inquiry into why teachers teach as they do is central to the long-term developmental process of learning to teach and understanding the complex nature of teaching.

---

1 *REASONING TEACHING: KEEPING A REFLECTIVE JOURNAL*

Many of the Investigations in this book will ask you to create entries in a reflective journal. Keeping a journal will enable you to explore your own knowledge and beliefs about teachers and teaching, gain insight into your own reasoning about teaching, and better understand your own teaching practices. Your reflective journal may remain private or it may become a springboard for discussions with classmates, fellow teachers, or your instructor. Ultimately, your reflective journal should become a personal record of your own journey into reasoning teaching.

The following Investigation has two parts. The first asks you to reflect on Emily's reasoning and reconceptualize her lesson in terms of your own conception of teachers and teaching. The second asks you to select a skill or concept in your own teaching and reflect on it from the multiple perspectives that exist in your professional landscape.

In your reflective journal:

A. Imagine that you are Emily, trying to decide how to teach this lesson on prewriting strategies for a freshman composition course. What would you think about as you plan this lesson? What would you do and why would you do it? How would you do things differently from the real Emily, and why?

In your reflective journal:

B. Now select a skill or concept that you are expected to teach. Reflect on this skill from your own personal experience. Have you had to use it? in what manner? where and when? What role do you believe it plays in language learning and/or learning?

Reflect on this skill from the perspective of your students. Do you think they may have used it? in what manner? where and when? If you're not sure, how might you find this out from them?

Reflect on this skill from the perspective of your school. Why do you think it is a part of the curriculum that you are supposed to teach? Why is it positioned in the curriculum as it is? How will your students be expected to use this skill once they leave your classroom? How might it fit into other skills your students are expected to master?

Reflect on this skill from a theoretical perspective. What role does it play in the learning and/or language-learning process?

With other teachers:

C. Describe how you have conceptualized this lesson and articulate your reasoning for why you would teach this lesson in this particular manner.

THE INTERPRETIVE AND SITUATED NATURE OF TEACHING

Ask any teacher and she or he will tell you that you can never teach the same thing the same way twice—what works with one group of students may fail with another. So for teachers, the notion that teaching means figuring out what to do about a particular topic, with a particular group of students, in a particular time and place, is not all that startling. What is startling is that most language teacher education programs have not embraced this view of teaching. On the contrary, most programs present teachers with a quantifiable amount of knowledge, usually in the form of general theories and methods that are characterized as being applicable to any language learning or teaching context. In addition, this knowledge tends to be oversimplified, decontextualized, compartmentalized into separate course offerings, and transmitted through passive instructional strategies such as course readings, lectures, exams, and term papers.

As a result, what teachers learn becomes what Whitehead (1929) defines as inert knowledge—that is, knowledge that can be recalled when one is explicitly asked to do so, but not used spontaneously in problem solving even though it is relevant. Spiro et al. claim that the oversimplification of complex knowledge or

monolithic representations of knowledge will too often leave their
holders facing situations for which their rigid "plaster-casts" simply
do not fit. The result is the often heard complaint of students:
"We weren't taught that." By which they mean that they weren't
taught *exactly* that. They lack the ability to use their knowledge
in new ways, the ability to think for themselves. (1987, p. 181)

I know this was the case in my own teacher education program. We offered
course work in Second Language Acquisition, Methodology, Applied Linguistics,
English Phonology and Syntax, and Cross-cultural and Classroom Communication. Not only were these courses taught independent of one another, our methods
of instruction followed the typical lecture, assigned readings, and term papers
found in most university settings. We did provide a practicum experience, but
we operated under the unrefuted assumption that our teachers would be able to
transfer what they learned in our courses into effective instructional practices
once they entered the classroom. We did make valorous attempts to contextualize our theory courses so that our teachers would recognize the relevance of theory for classroom practice. We had built-in reflective practices in which teachers
become investigators of their own teaching and kept logs of their learning experiences and reflective journals about their teaching experiences. They videotaped
their instruction and reflected on why they teach the way they do.

Despite all this, the futility of our efforts was never more clear to me than
when I investigated the experience of one of my own preservice teachers during
her TESOL practicum (Johnson, 1996a). This teacher had excellent grades in all
of her course work and by all traditional measures of competence was considered one of our best and brightest graduates. Yet it was painfully clear that we
had failed to provide this teacher with a realistic view of teaching that adequately prepared her to cope with the realities of the classroom. Instead, this teacher
had little, if any, procedural knowledge about the day-to-day operations of managing a second language classroom. She had inadequate knowledge about second language students. She was given little or no control over what or how she
would teach during the practicum. Finally, she had unrealistic expectations about
what the practicum would be like and what she could expect to gain from it.

I suspect that in most language teacher education programs, the particular
kinds of knowledge and the way in which such knowledge is presented to teachers remain vastly different from how teachers actually use their knowledge in
the classroom. This remains the status quo in language teacher education
because "teacher education is predicated on the assumption that knowing something in one context will convert into doing it in another" (Freeman, 1994, p. 1).
We assume that the oversimplified, decontextualized theories and methods of
language learning and teaching that teachers learn about will somehow turn
into complex ways of acting and interacting with a particular group of students
in a particular time and place. Anecdotal evidence of the nontransferability of
such knowledge is not hard to find. This same teacher wrote the following entry
in her teaching journal at the completion of her practicum experience:

In class [the university methods course] we talk about "the students"
as these generic things, like faceless blobs, that are always out there
waiting for us to teach them. But now when I think of students I see

faces and names, and personalities, and real people who have real experiences, and I know these people. I know what they like and don't like. I know how they will act and what they will say if I call on them. Now that I know them, I can teach them. Before, it was just a shot in the dark, but now I know what I'm aiming at. (Johnson, 1996a, p. 46)

Why did this teacher conclude her teacher education program and still not know what she was aiming at? In part it is because she had only just begun to experience the highly situated and interpretive nature of actual teaching. Packer and Winne suggest that an interpretivist view of teaching

must consider the fact that the activity and practices of teaching always take place in a setting that is already interpreted and understood; a setting, in fact, that has typically been designed and produced to support and sustain a particular mode of teaching-and-learning. [Thus] information the teacher thinks about is a joint function of what is in the place of teaching and what the teacher is capable of recognizing or perceiving about that place." (1995, p. 2).

While teaching is a highly situated activity, it is also a highly interpretive activity. Freeman characterizes teachers as

constantly involved in interpreting their worlds: they interpret their subject matter, their classroom context, and the people in it. These interpretations are central to their thinking and their actions. Classrooms and students are not just settings for implementing ideas; they are the frameworks of interpretation that teachers use for knowing: knowing when and how to act and react, what information to present or explain and how, when to respond or correct individual students, how to assess and reformulate what they have just taught and so on. (1996, p. 98).

Moreover, the knowledge teachers master in their teacher education programs is not situated within the social context where it is to be used, the interconnectedness of that knowledge is not made obvious, and teachers have virtually no opportunity to use that knowledge in the situated and interpretive ways required of real teachers in real classrooms. If we recognize teaching as a highly situated and interpretive activity, then knowing what to do in any classroom hinges on the robustness of teachers' reasoning.

ROBUST REASONING

Robust reasoning emerges within teachers themselves. Teachers are first and foremost people who come to the teaching profession with particular ways of understanding their experiences there. They hold certain beliefs, assumptions, and knowledge about what should and should not happen in classrooms. They have individual conceptions of teachers and teaching, particular views of students and learning, and individual ways of making sense of what they say and do in the classroom. If teachers are to develop robust reasoning, they must come to understand what they know and believe about teaching, the sources of their knowledge and beliefs, how they make sense of their own teaching, why they teach as they do, and how and why they rethink and change their teaching over time.

Robust reasoning also emerges through a process of looking beyond what teachers do in their classrooms to exploring the complex nature of the reasoning that shapes what they do. Understanding teachers' practices through their reasoning enables teachers to recognize the interrelationships between what they know and believe and what they do in their classrooms. It creates opportunities to explore the completeness of teachers' understandings of themselves, their students, and the places where they work. It enables teachers to recognize the flexibility with which they make use of those understandings, and to identify the instructional considerations they make use of as they teach. Understanding teachers' practices through their reasoning creates opportunities for teachers to recognize, refine, and expand their own reasoning in ways that encompass the socially constructed, highly contextualized, and interpretive nature of real teaching.

To do this, teachers must engage in critical reflection—reflection on themselves as teachers, on the lives of other teachers, on their own teaching practices, on the teaching practices of others, and on the places where teachers work. Using Dewey's (1933) definition of reflection as mental problem solving requiring active and deliberate consideration of action in light of any and all relevant knowledge and beliefs, critical reflection enables teachers to recognize how their knowledge and beliefs are tacitly embodied in their practices. However, critical reflection is not generally associated with the daily activities of teachers and, therefore, it is often difficult to sustain within teachers' professional lives. Fostering reflection requires ample time and supported opportunities, and it may be best carried out collaboratively so groups of teachers can examine their knowledge and beliefs, explore alternative views and approaches to classroom practice, and construct and reconstruct their understandings of and explanations for their own classroom practices over time. Hatton and Smith describe the use of "critical friend" dyads as a powerful strategy for fostering such reflection:

> It is a technique which can be structured to provide a safe environment within which self-revelation can take place. Also students are able to distance themselves from their actions, ideas, and beliefs, holding them up for scrutiny in the company of a peer with whom they are willing to take such risks. It creates an opportunity for giving voice to one's own thinking while at the same time being heard in a sympathetic but constructively critical way. (1995, p. 41)

In addition, teachers must engage in critical inquiry into teachers' classroom practices by exploring why teachers teach as they do. They must examine how teachers perceive and respond to what their students say and do. They must trace how teachers manage the dilemmas they face in the classroom. They must articulate to themselves and to others what constrains and persuades their reasoning and therefore their teaching behaviors. They must situate their abstract theoretical knowledge of learning and teaching within the familiar contexts of their own experiences as students and teachers. When teachers articulate why they teach the way they do, when they reflect on general theories and methods within the context of their own experiences and/or classrooms, and when they talk about their reasoning with others, it fosters the kind of sense making that enables them to develop robust reasoning.

Teachers who view themselves as life-long learners of teaching; who engage in sustained critical reflection and inquiry into their own knowledge and practices; who recognize that in teaching, it depends; and who can articulate what it depends on will develop complex, flexible, conceptual understandings of themselves, their students, their classrooms, and their schools, and will be able to use their knowledge in different ways, for different purposes, and in different instructional contexts, enabling them to provide truly effective teaching practices.

2 CRITICAL REFLECTION ON REASONING TEACHING

Well-remembered events are incidents or episodes that you observed and/or participated in within a school situation and consider, for your own reasons, especially salient or memorable. By recalling, analyzing, and sharing well-remembered events you are able to gain insight into the complex nature of reasoning teaching.

A. Select a well-remembered event that occurred during a past or your current teaching situation. As you recall this event, reflect on the most salient personal and professional experiences that may have influenced your perceptions of this event. In particular, reflect on your reasoning in this event. In other words, try to articulate why you did what you did and on what basis you made your decisions.

B. Write a two- to three-page description and analysis of this event. Include the following:

- A description of the event

- A description of your reasoning in this event (Why did you do what you did?)

- An analysis of your reasoning (On what basis did you do what you did?)

C. Share your well-remembered event with a group of teachers and/or your instructor:

- Discuss the similarities and/or differences found in the reasoning within these events

- Discuss what you learned from writing about this event

- Discuss what you learned from hearing about other teachers' well-remembered events

Suggested Readings

For much of their history, language teaching and language teacher education have been conceptualized around the notion of "methods." However, three recent *TESOL Quarterly* articles when read together offer alternative conceptions of what constitutes language teaching. N. S. Prabhu's article, "There is no best method—Why?" (*TESOL Quarterly* 24 (2): 161–176, 1990) critiques the notion of best method, suggesting that it is not the method, per se, that is good or bad, but teachers' interpretations and implementation of their own sense of plausibility that makes language teaching dynamic and alive. Along the same line, B. Kumaravadivelu (*TESOL Quarterly* 28 (1): 9–26, 1994) offers an alternative to the notion of method, arguing instead that teachers must develop open-ended strategic frameworks that are context-specific and needs-based. And finally, Mark Clarke's article, "The Dysfunctions of the Theory/Practice Discourse" (*TESOL Quarterly* 28 (1): 9–26, 1994) tackles the thorny issue of why teachers find the bulk of research and/or theory irrelevant to their work.

My own conception of teacher learning has been influenced by the research in cognitive psychology that explores the acquisition of advanced knowledge in ill-structured knowledge domains; in other words, professional contexts where learners must be able to apply what they know flexibly to fit the specific needs of those contexts. For a somewhat technical but fascinating view of this sort of human learning, I recommend the Rand Spiro et al. article "Knowledge Acquisition for Application: Cognitive Flexibility and Transfer in Complex Content Domains" (Mahwah, NJ: Lawrence Erlbaum Associates, *Executive control processes in reading,* 1987). Finally, within language teaching, Donald Freeman and Jack Richards' book *Teacher learning in language teaching* (New York: Cambridge University Press, 1996) offers a superb collection of research-based descriptive accounts of language teachers, language teaching, and language teachers learning to teach.

2

TEACHERS' KNOWLEDGE: A VIEW FROM THE INSIDE OUT

1 *REFLECTING ON YOUR INITIAL TEACHING EXPERIENCE*

Before you read about the nature of teachers' knowledge, I suggest that you do this Investigation. It will enable you to begin your exploration into the nature of teachers' knowledge from the inside out.

In your reflective journal:

A. Describe your very first teaching experience. What was memorable about it and why? How did you know what to do? How did you know what to say? Reflecting on this experience, what did you learn from it? Describe the ways in which this experience has shaped the type of teacher you are today.

THE INITIAL TEACHING EXPERIENCE

Most teachers hold vivid memories of their initial teaching experience. Vivid because it represents the first time they actually engaged in an activity with which they were keenly familiar, as students, yet strangely unfamiliar, as teachers. And vivid because most teachers realize that there is much more to teaching than they had ever imagined. Exploring your initial teaching experiences helps you understand the experiences that shape your initial conceptions of who you are as teachers, how you approach the activity of teaching, and why you aspire to teach the way you do.

KAREN: A LEGITIMATE DOG TRAINER

My first memories of teaching come from my adolescence, when as a fourteen-year-old semi-experienced dog trainer I was assigned a small group of adults who had registered for a 4-H dog obedience class. Anyone who has trained a dog—or any animal for that matter—knows it is not so much what the dog does or doesn't do that is important, but what the trainer does or doesn't do that signals to the dog what it should do. So there I was, surrounded by a group of nervous adults, most concerned that they themselves would look foolish as they conjoined, tugged, and stumbled around unknowingly with their beloved pets.

As a new teacher, I did what most new teachers do: I taught the way I had been taught. I explained that dogs by their very nature want to please their owners, but they need to be given consistent signals about what that entails. With my own well-trained sheltie at my left side, I modeled exactly what I wanted my students to do: I took one step forward, starting off on my left foot, and said my dog's name and the command "Heel." I took two more steps, slowly bringing my left foot forward last, pulling up slightly on her collar, and said, "Sit." I then praised her with a quick pat to her head and a positive "Good dog." I modeled this pattern several times, each time explaining exactly what I was doing and why, what was being signaled to my dog, and how I wanted her to respond. I then turned to the group of anxious adults and asked them to try this simple pattern on my command. I remember the feeling of true amazement when I called out the command "Heel" and every member of the group responded as I had modeled. Of course, the dogs did not respond in kind. Instead, most wandered away from their owners or charged ahead as if off on a new adventure.

As I recall this memory, I wonder how I knew what to say and do with this group of dog owners. How did I know that my students and their dogs would learn what I had taught them? How did I know how to make my instruction accessible to a variety of learning styles (and canine temperaments!). In a sense, I didn't—not consciously, at least—but I was very familiar and extremely comfortable with what should and should not happen in a dog obedience class. I had a powerful image to follow: that of my own mother, whose dog obedience classes I had attended for several years and who allowed me to be a legitimate participant in the social practices of dog training. It was this firsthand experience of actually training a dog that enabled me to know what to do and say to my very first group of students. In addition to firsthand experience, I had established a certain amount of credibility within my mother's dog training community, having entered and won several dog obedience competitions, beating out dog trainers twice my age. These successes enabled me to establish a certain amount of credibility, within myself and from others, since legitimate authorities—trial judges and other dog trainers—viewed me as a legitimate dog trainer.

If my first teaching experience had been with teaching languages, I might have become a very different sort of teacher. It's easy to "do things" in a dog obedience class. It's much harder to do things in a language classroom. Language classrooms tend to be places where you learn about language—at least, that was the bulk of my own school-based foreign language learning experiences. We learned about Spanish; we never did anything with Spanish. We memorized dialogues—"Hola, Isabelle. ¿Como estas? Muy bien, gracias. ¿Y tu?" is burned into my memory. Mostly we completed fill-in-the-blank grammar exercises, took dictation, or repeated phrases in unison. However, this "doing" versus "learning about" remains a salient characteristic of my own teaching. Every class I teach has some component that engages students in "doing" something. And to enable my students to do what I want them to do, I almost always provide some sort of explicit model that "shows" them exactly what they are expected to do and how they are to do it. I suppose I learn best from models and so that's how I teach.

FREDRIQUE: REALITY BITES, AND I LEARNED THE HARD WAY

I will never forget that very first day I stepped into my first classroom. The school had a reputation for being filled with the worst-disciplined students in that particular suburban area. I didn't know what I was in for before I walked into the room. The night before that first encounter I spent hours planning the day's lesson, and I even conferred with my colleagues on the best approach and materials to strike the students' fancy. I planned to teach "the perfect tenses." I had my roll-up chart, a colorful tense chart, and, of course, a Suggestopedia puppet in hand.

When I walked in, the students didn't even acknowledge my presence. I had to knock on the desk and say the greeting for the day. In response they just stared at me. It felt like they were scrutinizing every inch of me, and at that moment, I wanted the floor to open up and make me disappear from the face of the earth. Nervously, I began the lesson. I spoke perfect English. I took out the charts and hung them on the board. The class was silent. If a pin had dropped, it would have echoed in the room. No one broke away from his or her stare. But when I started to finger one student at random to respond to my questions, the rest of the class resumed their own activities (most of which were getting into arguments with their neighbors).

At that point I began to realize how inexperienced I was. All the mumbo-jumbo theories I had learned and memorized in college about wonderful learning behaviorism and classroom communication seemed inappropriate and useless. I had to think on my feet about how to resolve the conflicts between the students and try to channel their short attention spans into my well-crafted lesson. I was frustrated. The students began to speak with each other in Cantonese. I tried to speak in Malay. They didn't understand me. They ignored me. Thank goodness for a handful of students who sat in the front rows and who appeared to be more academically oriented than the rest. They managed to converse with me in Malay (using their limited knowledge of the language), and I carried on with teaching what I wanted to teach for the day.

That particular experience made a great imprint on my personal outlook on the teaching profession in general. Even if I knew all the theoretical constructs of language learning pedagogy, I was still handicapped by my limited classroom experience. There were too many disruptions that went on during that period, and I had to learn to deal with them immediately. Teaching is tough, I suppose, because the learning that I experienced as a student was always a sheltered environment. I went to the best schools and I had wonderful parents and teachers who supported my learning process one way or the other. When I faced the reality of an EFL classroom in a suburban area, however, my perfect mental picture of a language classroom suddenly broke into tiny pieces. Perhaps I was just another novice teacher who wanted to create a perfect learning environment for my students. I know now that reality bites, and I learned that the hard way.

---

2 *COMPARING INITIAL TEACHING EXPERIENCES*

Use your journal entry from Investigation 1 to relate to these teachers' initial teaching experiences. Doing so will enable you to see similarities and differences in how teachers' initial teaching experiences shape how they conceptualize themselves as teachers and how they come to understand their own teaching.

In your reflective journal:

A. Relate Karen's and Fredrique's experiences to your own initial teaching experience. How are their experiences similar to or different from yours? What are the most salient aspects of your own experience that you share with these teachers? Why do you think you share them? How have these experiences shaped your conception of yourself as a teacher?

With other teachers:

B. Discuss the similarities and/or differences you have found in your initial teaching experiences. How have these initial teaching experiences shaped your conception of yourselves as teachers? What have you learned from hearing about other teachers' first teaching experiences?

DIVERGENT VIEWS OF TEACHERS' KNOWLEDGE

As both Karen's and Fredrique's recollections suggest, much of what teachers know about teaching comes from their real-life experiences inside and outside the classroom. But this is not the traditional view of teachers' knowledge that has dominated educational research over the past thirty years. In fact, much of the past educational research on teaching considered teachers' knowledge to be something that was almost external to the teacher. In other words, teachers' knowledge was assumed to be an extended body of empirically derived theories and facts based on research on how students learn and what effective teachers do. Based on the assumption that effective teachers produced high student achievement, expertise in teaching was characterized as systematic, codifiable, observable teaching behaviors that integrated subject matter knowledge with classroom knowledge, with the final outcome being student learning (Berliner, 1986). Given this view of teachers' knowledge, it was assumed that what new teachers needed to know was generated by researchers using empirical observational and research tools, and must be presented to new teachers in the form of general theories, assertions, and methods of instruction that could be explained, investigated, and transferred into any teaching context.

For teacher education programs, this meant that new teachers should be immersed, as learners, in a particular subject matter such as literature, math, science, or languages, and at the same time trained to replicate effective models of instruction. Novice teachers, like students, were considered blank slates on which knowledge about teaching was to be imprinted. This external view of teachers' knowledge was—and still is—so pervasive that those who enter teacher education programs often assume that there is one best method of teaching that can be learned, mastered, and applied to any group of students in any classroom.

The limitations of this view of teachers' knowledge are obvious. It fails to recognize that teachers enter teacher education programs with a wealth of knowledge about teachers and teaching based largely on their experiences as learners both inside and outside the classroom. And it fails to recognize that what teachers do learn in their teacher education programs will most likely be filtered through their prior experiences and preexisting beliefs, which act as intuitive screens (Goodman, 1988) through which they view themselves as teachers and make sense of their own teaching.

Based on more recent research on what teachers actually know, how they think about their teaching, and why they teach the way they do, an alternative view of teachers' knowledge has emerged from educational research. This view characterizes teachers' knowledge as internal to the teacher, recognizing teachers' prior experiences, personal values, and individual purposes as being related to and informing their professional knowledge (Elbaz, 1983; Connelly & Clandinin, 1988).

This view argues that what teachers know about teaching is inseparable from who they are as people and what they do in their classrooms. Therefore, it recognizes teachers' knowledge as largely experiential, as something that is socially constructed out of the experiences and classrooms from which teachers have come and in which they teach.

Experiential knowledge, then, is the accumulation of our real-life experiences, which shape who we are and how we perceive and respond to the world around us. Others have called this sort of knowledge one's personal history, or the experiences that model the educational thinking of teachers (Feiman-Nemser & Buchmann, 1985).

Bound up in teachers' personal histories and experiential knowledge are their experiences as students in classrooms. Lortie believes that much of what teachers know about teaching comes from what he calls the *apprenticeship of observation* (1975). Having spent anywhere from twelve to twenty years in classrooms watching teachers teach, most of us are extremely familiar with what goes on there. Our memories from our days as students may include a repertoire of teaching strategies with which we then felt comfortable, assumptions about how students learn based on our own learning styles and strategies, and a bias toward certain types of instructional materials with which we became familiar. However, Lortie also claims that these memories are asymmetrical, since they formulate a conception of teaching based on perceptions as students rather than as teachers.

> They [students] are not privy to the teacher's private intentions and
> personal reflections on classroom events. Students rarely participate
> in selecting goals, making preparations, or post mortem analysis. . . .
> It is improbable that many students learn to see teaching in a means-
> ends frame or that they normally take an analytic stance toward
> it. . . . What students learn about teaching, then, is intuitive and
> imitative rather than explicit and analytical. (Lortie, 1975, p. 62)

Acknowledging the power of teachers' apprenticeship of observation, Buchmann argues that teachers acquire their teaching knowledge by participating in the usages and social customs associated with experiences of learning and teaching in all walks of life. Characterizing it as "the informal occupational socialization of teachers" (1987, p. 152), Buchmann argues that much of teachers' knowledge is acquired through acquaintance, since the inner nature of teaching is not readily available and, therefore, the practices of teaching tend to be carried out more on the basis of imitation than of understanding and follow unchallenged common sense principles.

In this sense the apprenticeship of observation can be both a blessing and a curse. The combination of teachers' memories and experiences as students enables them to function immediately in the classroom, but at the same time the imprint of such memories may be difficult for teachers to overcome and, in fact, may tend to support a conservatism in teaching, promulgating the notion that *teachers teach the way they were taught.* Feiman-Nemser and Buchmann describe the process of learning to teach as overcoming the pitfalls of our experiential knowledge. They argue that novice teachers need to appreciate how "their personal history and experience of schooling influence their perceptions of classrooms in a way that makes it difficult to see alternatives" (1985, p. 63). For Fredrique, what had worked for her as a student did not work with the rambunctious group of adolescents in her first classroom. Furthermore, since she had no alternative experiences as a student, she had little to fall back on when her lesson plan went awry.

It seems obvious that if the apprenticeship of observation has such a powerful impact on teachers' knowledge, it must also have a powerful impact on reasoning teaching, in effect forming the basis for how teachers conceptualize, construct explanations for, and carry out their classroom practices. And if this is the case, then time spent exploring your apprenticeship of observation is time well spent.

THE POWER OF THE APPRENTICESHIP OF OBSERVATION

For most teachers, the apprenticeship of observation encompasses two types of memories. The first is our memories as students: how we as students were expected to talk and act and what we learned from the experience of being students. The second is our memories of our former teachers: what these teachers did and said and how they approached teaching and learning. Unknowingly, these memories become the basis of our initial conceptions of ourselves as teachers, influence our view of students, formulate the foundation of our reasoning, and act as the justifications for our teaching practices. Interestingly, these memories also seem to have a lasting impact on the kind of teacher we each aspire to be.

ANNE: SCHOOL LEARNING VERSUS REAL LEARNING

My memory of school in general—which I never liked, so I don't know why I'm a teacher—is that you're totally at the mercy of the teacher. You must do what the teacher says and when the teacher says it. And even if the teacher is wrong, there's nothing you can do about it. And if you get interested in something, you can't pursue it because the teacher is now on to something else. And I've always enjoyed learning but rarely have I enjoyed learning it in school. But I have enjoyed learning it with teachers who allowed us to pursue our own interests, allowed us to sometimes work in groups, work on our own, and were interested in what you had to say.

My strongest memory of a teacher was one of my history professors in college, who, for the first time, taught me that it's all right to think. He never asked the type of question where you repeat what you just read, or you repeat what he just said. It was always, "Well, now that you know that, what do you think about this problem?" And so we were forced to think for ourselves: "If this had happened in a different way, what would have been the result of that?" And I think it's had a great influence on me as a teacher, because I want my students to think. We have final exams in this school, and I tell them that they're not going to remember what they did in this class. As a matter of fact, I know that for a fact because I teach the same kids in seventh and eighth grades, and I know they don't remember what I taught them last year. But if they can learn how to think, that will stand them in good stead for the rest of their lives. So that is what I try to do.

I see myself as a facilitator, as someone who's here to take the students and help them to know what their own abilities are, and to encourage them to go as far as they can with those abilities. Not as someone who has to teach a certain set curriculum, or I don't feel that there's a certain amount of material that has to be covered every year, or if this lesson has to change due to something else, that's going to change things. I will feel badly if, at the end, the kids don't have more self-confidence, feel better about themselves, have more interest in different types of things, and be able to feel that next year they can do better.

ELSA: WHEN WILL SCHOOL BE OVER SO I CAN DO WHAT I WANT TO DO?

Around the time of entering junior high school, my feelings about "education" took a turn for the worse. I still enjoyed some of the work I was asked to do, but more of it became a boring chore for me. I especially hated being in that same building all day, following basically the same daily routine. I felt restricted by having very little control over how my time was spent. In fact, I remember resenting, to some degree, the fact that I had to be there when I felt that, often, there were much more productive ways I could have been spending my time. But I was always looking forward—to the end of the day, so I could enjoy my after-school activities, and to the end of twelfth grade, when I thought I would be free. I wouldn't say that my junior high and high school days were negative—just that they did not realize their potential. Because of this experience, I aspire for the classes I teach to be more than just stepping-stones to more important goals. Of course, most courses will contribute to the realization of some larger goal, but there is no reason that they should not be engaging, challenging, and valuable in the present also. I strongly believe in working to make classes personally and presently relevant for students, and giving them enough freedom of expression and movement so they do not feel restrained as I did in high school. The goal of education is to invite engagement and growth, not inhibit them.

One of the reasons I was anxious for the precious time, 3:12 P.M., to arrive during junior high and high school was so that I could leave school and go to dance class. During these years I was seriously involved with a modern dance school, which I attended almost daily. The school was directed and operated entirely by one woman. This woman was clearly a teacher. She helped us, her students, to greater understandings of ourselves and our world, directed the activities which would promote this goal, and had clear expectations of the tasks we should engage in to practice our skills and reveal our development. But she never danced herself.

Instead of actually demonstrating the skills she wanted us to acquire, she created an environment rich in multiple forms of stimulation, and provided enough direction that we could generate the movements and ideas ourselves. She devoted each year to the study of a particular period in dance or art history—such as Primitivism, Impressionism, and Minimalism. We would examine works of art from the period, listen to music representative of the period, watch videotapes of dances that had been inspired by the period, and discuss our interpretations. At the end of each year, each student was responsible for performing a dance based on her year-long consideration of this period and how it related to her life at the time.

Although each step in the choreography process was closely monitored and guided, each student had a tremendous amount of freedom in creating her dance. For example, I would be responsible for choosing my own music, my theme within the period, and the movements I would use in the dance. After the initial stages of work, students would critique each other's dances verbally and in writing and receive extensive feedback and individual "coaching" from our teacher. I think of this experience as sort of a model of one way education can function successfully to facilitate the development of students' understandings in a positive and gratifying way. Participating in the dance school was not easy. It required a tremendous amount of time, discipline, and mental and physical effort. And yet the students participated willingly and happily. There were no grades, no promises of a successful future, no hope of societal prestige, and no penalties for not participating.

3 *Exploring the Apprenticeship of Observation*

As modeled by Anne and Elsa, the following Investigation will enable you to explore your own apprenticeship of observation: determining for yourself how your memories of being a student and of your former teachers have shaped both your conception of yourself as a teacher and the kind of teacher you aspire to be.

In a group:

A. Describe your most memorable teacher (positive or negative). What was memorable about him or her and why? Share your description with your group.

B. Describe your most memorable classroom teaching experience (positive or negative). What was memorable about it and why? Share your description with your group.

C. Describe what has influenced you the most as a teacher. How did you learn to teach? Share your description with your group.

D. Based on your descriptions, create a visual depiction of a typical teacher you've had. Describe your visual depiction to your group. Next create a visual depiction of the type of teacher you want to be. Then describe your visual depiction to your group.

THE LIMITATIONS OF THE APPRENTICESHIP OF OBSERVATION

The question that teachers often ask me after I ask them to walk down memory lane is, "So what? Now that I have reflected on my memories of being a student and my former teachers, how will this help me figure out what to do on Monday morning?" My initial response is that it probably won't—not directly, anyway. But if they were to reflect on what they thought about as they planned their lessons, how they structured their lessons, what kinds of learning activities they created, and how they acted and interacted with their students during their lessons, they would probably find evidence that certain dimensions of their apprenticeship of observation are tacitly embodied in their classroom practices. Moreover, given that the apprenticeship of observation enables teachers to function immediately in classrooms but can also limit them to teaching the way they were taught, then moving beyond the apprenticeship of observation is an important step in the developmental process of learning to teach.

A few years ago I worked with two teachers who candidly described the difficulties they experienced overcoming their apprenticeship of observation. After watching herself teach on videotape, the first teacher, Gretchen, expressed her frustration with her own instructional behavior:

> It's been really frustrating to watch myself do the old behaviors and not know how to "fix it" at the time. I know now that I don't want to teach like this. I don't want to be this kind of teacher, but I don't have any other experiences. It's like I just fall into the trap of teach-

ing like I was taught and I don't know how to get myself out of that mode. I think I still need more role models of how to do this, but it's up to me to really strive to *apply* what I believe in when I'm actually teaching. (Johnson, 1994, p. 446)

The second teacher, Sylvia, explained after watching her videotape:

I desperately want their experiences in my class to be meaningful and useful; that is something I rarely experienced as a student. But, I'm the teacher here and I'm supposed to teach them something, right? One part of me wants to let them just take off, because that's when they really express themselves, but then I think about my responsibility as the teacher, and have to pull back and make sure we are going somewhere. Inside I know learning goes on regardless of what I do, in fact, maybe in spite of what I do, but I also feel like I have this huge responsibility to my students, to teach them something, so I find myself slipping back into that traditional teacher-mode. (Johnson, 1994, p. 449)

Both Gretchen and Sylvia had powerful images of their experiences as students and memories of their former teachers. Gretchen found herself teaching as she had been taught, despite the fact that she did not want to teach this way. Sylvia had a strong image of what a teacher should do, despite the realization that allowing students to engage in meaningful self-directed communication was, in this particular instance, probably more beneficial than any sort of teacher-directed instruction. For both of these teachers, the apprenticeship of observation retained a powerful grip over how they taught. Moreover, both teachers seemed stunned by this realization. Gretchen and Sylvia needed to realize the limitations of their apprenticeship of observation in order to move beyond it as their sole model of teaching.

As it did for Gretchen and Sylvia, the apprenticeship of observation acts as an indelible imprint on most teachers' lives and minds, influencing their knowledge, their reasoning, and their teaching practices. It forms the basis for how teachers conceptualize their knowledge and practice, a basis that is in all likelihood incomplete and insufficient for the development of robust reasoning teaching.

TEACHERS' PROFESSIONAL KNOWLEDGE

Obviously, teachers possess a great deal of experiential knowledge, based largely on their prior learning and teaching experiences. However, this knowledge relates to and informs their professional knowledge, since what teachers know about teaching cannot be separated from who they are as people and what they do in their classrooms. Connelly and Clandinin capture this view of teachers and teaching in their definition of the term *personal practical knowledge*:

A term designed to capture the idea of experience in a way that allows us to talk about teachers as knowledgeable and knowing persons. Personal practical knowledge is in the teacher's past experience, in the teacher's present mind and body, and in the future plans and actions. Personal practical knowledge is found in the teacher's practice. (1988, p. 25)

They claim that personal practical knowledge is embedded in and inseparable from teachers' practice since it aids teachers in responding to new situations and is reformulated through experience and reflection.

Combined with and understood through teachers' experiential knowledge is what Shulman (1986) has characterized as teachers' professional knowledge. Teachers' professional knowledge includes four general areas: subject matter knowledge, general pedagogical knowledge, pedagogical content knowledge, and knowledge of context. These areas of teachers' professional knowledge are considered to have a direct impact on how teachers represent their subject matter content—in other words, what and how they teach.

Subject matter knowledge includes knowledge of the major facts and concepts in a subject area, as well as its major paradigms; how the area is organized; its fundamental theories, claims, and truths; and central questions of further inquiry. *General pedagogical knowledge* represents general knowledge about teaching, including beliefs and skills related to general principles of curriculum and instruction, learners and learning, and classroom management, that cut across subject areas. By combining subject matter knowledge and general pedagogical knowledge, Shulman characterizes an additional component of teachers' professional knowledge, *pedagogical content knowledge*. Shulman describes pedagogical content knowledge as "the blending of content and pedagogy into an understanding of how particular topics, problems, or issues are organized, represented, and adapted to the diverse interests and abilities of learners, and presented for instruction" (1986, p. 8). This concept includes a combination of knowledge related to the purposes for teaching a particular topic, students' understandings or misunderstandings of the topic, a host of curricular materials available to teach the topic, and specific strategies and representations that teachers use to make the topic comprehensible to students. Finally, *knowledge of context* includes the ecology of learning in the classroom, thus the context-specific knowledge that teachers use to adapt their instruction to the demands of the specific school setting and/or individual students within the unique context of their classrooms.

Within Shulman's model of teachers' professional knowledge, we can assume that language teachers enter teacher education programs with a great deal of knowledge about the language they are supposed to teach. This subject matter knowledge may consist of their tacit knowledge of the language, as well as any explicit knowledge they may have learned about the language through both formal and informal study. In addition, we can assume that language teachers hold certain assumptions about the nature of the language learning process and of second language learners. This general pedagogical knowledge may be based on a combination of their own experiences as second language learners or memories of their own teachers, as well as knowledge from their professional course work on, for example, theories of second language acquisition, methods of second language instruction, and language learners' styles and strategies.

We can also assume that language teachers have or will eventually learn a variety of ways in which they can represent the language so that it is comprehensible to their students. Again, this pedagogical content knowledge will likely be a combination of their own experiences as students and second language learners, as well as of what they know about how second languages are learned and how they should be taught. Finally, we can assume that language teachers will enter the classroom with some knowledge of both the ecology of learning in second language classrooms and the unique culture of classrooms, based on both their prior experiences as students and memories of their own teachers.

Overall, teachers' knowledge consists of a combination of experiential and professional knowledge that shapes teachers' reasoning and is tacitly embodied in their classroom practices. Using the term "knowing-in-action," Schon (1983, 1987) claims that teachers bring their experiential and professional knowledge to the classroom, although it may not be articulated, and use it to make sense of both their own and their students' behaviors. "Knowing-in-action" is dynamic in that teachers respond to each action with adjustments made in response to the context of that moment.

Schon also stresses the importance of reflection in the development of teachers' knowledge, since teachers can reflect on an action in order to evaluate how their "knowing-in-action" has contributed to the success of that action. Moreover, such reflection can occur during the act of teaching, otherwise known as "reflection-in-action," in which teachers use their tacit knowledge to make sense of and respond to an instructional situation spontaneously. Knowing-in-action and reflection-in-action thus represent tacit aspects of teachers' knowledge and reflect how that knowledge is reasoned and becomes realized during actual classroom teaching.

Thus, teachers' knowledge comes from the inside out. It represents both experiential and professional knowledge about teachers, teaching, learning, and students, the configuration of which will be idiosyncratic since differences in teachers' apprenticeship of observation, educational experiences, and teaching and learning experiences help to formulate the foundation for their reasoning. Ultimately, teachers' knowledge is tacitly embodied in their practices since it functions as the foundation for reasoning teaching.

---

4 *TEACHERS' AUTOBIOGRAPHIES*

All teachers have views of teaching and learning that are implicit in their practices but are rarely articulated. Writing an autobiography can help you capture the richness of your prior experiences and come to understand the complexity of your understandings of teachers, teaching, and learning.

Your autobiography should be a combination of reflections on your prior experiences and beliefs, a critical analysis of those experiences and beliefs, and the application of your insights to your current or future teaching practices. Consider the following as you construct your autobiography:

A. Reflection

- Memories and impressions of yourself as a student, of your former teachers, as a second language learner (in/out of the classroom), of your teacher preparation program, and of yourself as a teacher

- Beliefs and assumptions about how second languages are learned and how they should be taught
- Beliefs and assumptions about the roles of teacher and students in second language teaching and learning

B. Critical analysis

- Conceptions of how your prior experiences and beliefs shape you as a teacher and a learner
- Dimensions about yourself that you recognize and wish to maintain in your teaching and learning
- Dimensions about yourself that you recognize and wish to alter in your teaching and learning
- Dimensions about teaching and learning that represent your greatest challenge(s)

C. Application

- Description of a critical teaching or learning incident that encapsulates you as a teacher or learner
- How you understood the incident, how you responded to it, and how your understanding of and response to this incident reflect your conceptions of yourself as a teacher or a learner

D. Share your autobiography with a group of teachers and/or your instructor

- Discuss the similarities and differences among the autobiographies
- Discuss what you learned from writing your autobiography

---

5 *COLLABORATIVE AUTOBIOGRAPHIES*

Participating in the development of collaborative autobiographies creates an opportunity for groups of teachers to reflect on and write about their personal and professional histories and the impact of their histories on how they make sense of and participate in their current teaching situations. Through collaborative reflection, teachers can come to understand how they evolve, develop, and change their experiential and professional knowledge about teaching.

A. Establish a group of three to four teachers who are committed to meeting on a regularly scheduled basis over the course of several weeks. Group members will be required to bring written descriptions and reflections to each meeting for exchange and discussion. Each meeting will close with time allotted for continued written reflection.

B. Meeting #1:

Exchange and discuss written descriptions of the contexts in which you are currently teaching. Describe the institutional philosophy, the school personnel, the school's role in the community, the makeup of the student body, and any other information relevant to your teaching situations.

C. Meeting #2:

Exchange and discuss written descriptions of the instructional strategies and/or methodologies you use on a daily basis in your teaching. Describe details about the curriculum you are required to cover.

D. Meeting #3:

Exchange and discuss written reflections on your past personal and professional experiences that might help you and other group members better understand how you make sense of your current teaching practices.

E. Meeting #4:

Prior to this meeting, construct your own autobiography, based on a combination of your written descriptions and reflections and the discussions that have occurred during the first three meetings. Your autobiography should be a combination of reflections on your prior experiences and beliefs, a critical analysis of those experiences and beliefs, and the application of your insights to your current or future teaching practices. Exchange autobiographies with the other group members and discuss what you learned from writing your autobiography collaboratively.

---

6 TEACHERS' LIFE STORIES

Stories written by teachers represent the richness of teachers' ways of knowing and understanding. They capture the essence of teachers' experiences and make them accessible to readers both within and beyond the classroom. Oral book talks give you an opportunity to share, in an informal way, teachers' stories about teaching, learning, students, and life in the classroom.

A. Oral book talks should be given in small groups, each lasting between ten and fifteen minutes. Specific roles should be assigned for both the presenter and the listeners (see below). A list of possible books is given; however, teachers should be encouraged to select books that reflect teachers' experiences that are most closely related to their own.

B. Procedures for oral book talks:

Role of the presenter:

- Summarize the main focus of the book (i.e., the author's main point(s), premise, argument)
- Discuss new insights you gained from reading the book
- Provide critical analysis of the book (your concerns and/or criticisms)

- Give reasons why you would recommend this book to someone else

Role of the listeners:
- Ask questions, make comments, ask for clarification
- Describe (on paper) what you understand to be the "residual message" from this book talk
- Take note (on paper) of two or three critical points about the book that make it particularly relevant for your developing understanding of teaching

C. Book talks can also be completed in writing and exchanged among teachers. Written book talks should include the same criteria as oral book talks.

Book talk citation list

Ashton-Warner, S. 1963. *Teacher.* New York: Simon & Schuster.

Brookfield, Stephen. 1995. *Becoming a critically reflective teacher.* San Francisco, CA: Jossey-Ross.

Collins, Marva. 1992. *Ordinary children, extraordinary teachers.* Norfolk, VA: Hampton Roads.

Corcoran, John. 1994. *The teacher who couldn't read.* Colorado Springs, CO: Focus on the Family Publishing.

Freire, Pablo. 1986. *Pedagogy of the oppressed.* New York: Continuum.

Fu, Danling. 1995. *My trouble is my English: Asian students and the American dream.* Portsmouth, NH: Boynton/Cook.

Haley, M. A. 1982. *Battleground: The autobiography of Margaret A. Haley,* R. L. Reid (ed.). Urbana: University of Illinois Press.

Hayden, T. 1980. *One child.* New York: Avon.

hooks, bell. 1994. *Teaching to transgress: Education as the practice of freedom.* New York: Routledge.

Johnson, L. 1995. *The girls in the back of the class.* New York: St. Martin's Press.

Keizer, G. 1988. *No place but here: A teacher's vocation in a rural community.* New York: Viking Press

Kohl, Herbert. 1967. *36 Children.* New York: Plume Books.

Kohl, Herbert. 1984. *Growing minds: On becoming a teacher.* New York: Harper Torchbooks.

Kohl, Herbert. 1994. *I won't learn from you and other thoughts on creative maladjustments.* New York: John Hopkins University Press.

McDonald, Joseph. 1992. *Teaching: Making sense of an uncertain craft.* New York: Teachers College Press.

O'Reilley, Mary Rose. 1993. *The peaceable classroom.* Portsmouth, NH: Boyton/Cook Heinemann.

Paley, Vivian Gussin. 1979. *White teacher.* Cambridge, MA: Harvard University Press.

Paley, Vivian Gussin. 1990. *The boy who would be a helicopter.* Cambridge, MA: Harvard University Press.

Paley, Vivian Gussin. 1995. *Kwanzaa and me.* Cambridge, MA: Harvard University Press.

Paley, Vivian Gussin. 1997. *The girl with the brown crayon.* Cambridge, MA: Harvard University Press.

Perry, Theresa, and James Fraser (eds.). 1993. *Freedom's plan: Teaching in the multicultural classroom.* New York: Routledge.

Smith, Frank. 1986. *Insult to intelligence, the bureaucratic invasion of our classrooms.* Portsmouth, NH: Heinemann.

Wigginton, E. 1986. *Sometimes a shining moment: The Foxfire experience.* Garden City, NY: Doubleday.

Suggested Readings

The book to read if you really want to understand the notion of the "apprenticeship of observation" is Dan Lortie's *Schoolteacher: A sociological study* (Chicago, IL: University of Chicago Press, 1975). He gives us a fascinating look at life inside the lives and minds of teachers. For a language teacher eduction perspective, I recommend Kathi Bailey's et.al chapter, "The Language Learner's Autobiography: Examining the 'Apprenticeship of Observation'" (New York: Cambridge University Press, *Teacher learning in language teaching*, 1996).

The use of narratives or stories to explore teachers' knowledge is well documented in the general educational literature. Kathy Carter's article "The place of story in the study of teaching and teacher education" (*Educational Researcher* 22 (1): 5–12, 1993) provides a comprehensive overview of this research and its implications for teacher education. F. Michael Connelly and D. Jean Clandinin's book *Teachers as curriculum planners: Narratives as experience* (New York: Teachers College Press, 1988) also provides an excellent example of how narratives can be used to understand teachers and teaching and as a means of empowering teachers to construct their own professional development learning experiences.

Of course, examples of actual stories from teachers' real lives abound in the popular press. Some of the best and most accessible are Herbert Kohl's *36 Children* (New York: Plume Books, 1967), *Growing minds: On becoming a teacher* (New York: Harper Torchbooks, 1984), *I won't learn from you and other thoughts on creative maladjustments* (Baltimore, MD: John Hopkins University Press, 1994) and any of Vivian Gussin Paley's books; but in particular, *The boy who would be a helicopter* (Cambridge, MA: Harvard University Press, 1990), *White teacher* (Cambridge, MA: Harvard University Press, 1979) *Kwanzaa and me* (1995, Harvard University Press) or *The girl with the brown crayon* (Cambridge, MA: Harvard University Press, 1997). Finally, for a very accessible look at the relationship between narrative and intelligence, I recommend Roger Schank's book *Tell me a story: Narrative and intelligence* (Chicago, IL: Northwestern University Press, 1990).

3

TEACHERS' BELIEFS:
THE ROCK WE STAND ON

What are teachers' beliefs and how do they influence teachers' reasoning? Broadly defined, our beliefs shape our representation of reality and guide both our thoughts and our behaviors. Rokeach describes a belief system "as having represented within it, in some organized psychological but not necessarily logical form, each and every one of a person's countless beliefs about physical and social reality" (1968, p. 2). Beliefs have a cognitive, an affective, and a behavioral component and therefore act as influences on what we know, feel, and do. All human perception is influenced by beliefs, influencing the ways in which events are understood and acted on.

Teachers' beliefs can be thought of as a belief substructure that interrelates with all other beliefs; they have a filtering effect on everything that teachers think about, say, and do in classrooms. Pajares characterizes teachers' beliefs as having

> stronger affective and evaluative components than knowledge and
> that affect typically operates independently of the cognition associ-
> ated with knowledge. Knowledge of a domain differs from feelings
> about a domain. [Moreover,] knowledge system information is
> semantically stored, whereas, beliefs reside in episodic memory with
> material drawn from experience or cultural sources of knowledge
> transmission—what some have called folklore. (1992, pp. 309–310)

The strong affective and evaluative component of teachers' beliefs makes them seem more inflexible and less open to critical examination (Nespor, 1987). When teachers enter professional development programs at either the pre-service or the in-service level, they bring with them an accumulation of experiences that manifest themselves in beliefs that tend to be quite stable and rather resistant to change. Despite professional course work and practical field experiences, teachers' beliefs tend to remain unchanged regardless of the context within which they teach. Goodman characterizes teachers' beliefs as intuitive screens that act as a filter through which teachers make sense of new information about teaching:

> Once students [novice teachers] entered the program, these intuitive
> screens gave them an orientation point from which they made sense
> out of the activities and ideas presented to them. When exposed to
> new ideas or experiences, students tended to act first on an intuitive
> rather than an intellectual level. No matter how logical or sound the

idea seemed, if it directly contradicted a student's intuitive screen, it was usually rejected. (1988, p. 121)

These intuitive screens are used to "read" situations; interpret new information; and decide what is possible, realistic, or even proper. Since teachers' beliefs tend to be grounded in powerful episodic memories from prior learning and teaching experiences, they may reflect an extremely narrow view of teachers and teaching, and thus limit the range of instructional considerations and classroom practices that teachers are willing or able to consider. Once beliefs are formed, individuals have a tendency to build explanations around those beliefs, regardless of whether such explanations are accurate or are mere inventions (Pajares, 1992). In fact, teachers often use whatever justifications are necessary to appear congruent with their beliefs, and turn conflicting evidence into support for their beliefs, even when beliefs contradict one another (Nisbett & Ross, 1980). Yet Kennedy argues that if teachers' beliefs are to shift at all, they must have something to shift to:

Teachers need to be provoked to question their experiences and to question the beliefs that are based on those experiences. Provocation is most likely to occur in conjunction with vivid portraits of alternative models of teaching and a stimulus that focuses teachers' attention on the difference between this example and the teachers' tacit model of teaching. (1991, p. 9)

Given this characterization of teachers' beliefs, we can assume that they are inextricably complex, grounded in emotionally laden episodic memories from prior experiences, relatively stable and resistant to change, yet instrumental in shaping how teachers interpret what goes on in their classrooms and how they will react and respond to that. Teachers' beliefs have a powerful impact on the nature of teachers' reasoning since the ways in which teachers come to conceptualize themselves as teachers and develop explanations for their own classroom practices tend to be filtered through their beliefs.

---

1 *Beliefs About Second Language Learning and Teaching*

Investigations

Before you read examples of teachers' beliefs about language learning and teaching, I suggest that you do this Investigation. It will enable you to begin to think about your own beliefs about second language teachers, second language learning, and second language teaching, all of which will shape the way you think about your own teaching.

In your reflective journal:

A. Reflect on and answer the following questions: What does it mean to be an effective second language teacher? How do you think second languages are learned? What do you see as the most important factors in learning a second language? How do you think second languages should be taught? What should be the role of the teacher? What kinds of language learning experiences do you think a second language teacher should provide?

KEN: STRETCHING KIDS' MINDS

I think an effective second language teacher creates academic learning situations where kids can stretch their minds. At the same time that they are stretching their knowledge, they're stretching their minds to be able to deal with future knowledge in a more sophisticated way or in a more competent way. I think second languages are learned in natural communicative contexts. I think the natural approach, from my experiences teaching elementary school children, shows me that children learn languages much faster—or people in general, I think, when they're in the country where it's learned because all of the communication contexts are natural. If I walked into a college lecture and I just sat there, I wouldn't understand what I was hearing, even if I sat for a hundred hours, because there is no comprehension with what you're hearing.

So I think there needs to be comprehensible input, and I think there needs to be the context to stretch thinking and to stretch learning, and to be able to help kids to build a base to become successful learners later in their lives. One of the things that the teacher has to provide is a sense of security in the form of social limits, behavioral limits that kids clearly understand within the context of that environment. That there's security, that there's safety, that there's learning, that there's happiness, that there's caring from the teacher and amongst the children, and if there's bumping into that wall, then there are consequences, and everybody knows what they are. I think one of the rules of any teacher of children is to help children understand why there are limits, what they are, and that there can be happiness in classrooms.

ANNE: START WITH THE STUDENTS YOU HAVE

I don't think being an effective second language teacher is any different from being an effective any other kind of teacher; I think it's exactly the same thing. You need to start with the students that you have and what they need to do and how best to make them enjoy what they're doing, want to do it, and do it. I think especially with teenagers—but at any age, if people aren't interested in what they're doing, if they don't see a reason why they need to do it, if they don't understand what you want them to do, they aren't going to do well. I think that students feel a need to express themselves. So, therefore, the activities need to be realistic. When we are teaching beginners, we use many, many games. We use games constantly, because at this age they are shy. With different cultures sometimes they don't want to speak unless they're sure it's right. But, if they're playing a game and they want to beat you, they won't know they're talking. And, without knowing it, they are learning. Then, as you get to a higher level, they have to see the need for that.

And, therefore, the way I have the program set up here, I teach social studies, and it is instead of their other social studies class, it really is social studies. They're getting a grade in it, they feel a need to do it, it's what all the other kids are doing, and I try to have the subject be as close to what the other kids are doing as possible. I think you have to use age-appropriate activities, regardless of what the book says. And you have to be culturally aware. There are students from various cultures who behave or think in different ways, and you have to be able to assimilate that and accept it, and, perhaps, show them things are done in America a little bit differently so they will be able to fit in.

ELIZABETH: ADJUSTING TO STUDENTS' NEEDS

A good teacher is able to adjust to the needs of the students. For example, it isn't good, I think, to just push on relentlessly in a classroom so that you can get your lesson plan done. I think that you have to be able to continually reevaluate and respond to what's happening in the classroom. You often have to make spur-of-the-moment-adjustments and decisions. I think motivation plays a big part in learning languages. Whatever your motivation can be, it could be that you're in a foreign country and you need the language to communicate with the society, to fit in with the society. It could be that your husband speaks that language. It could be that you just like learning languages. It could be that you're planning to travel. It doesn't matter, as long as you have motivation. If you don't have any motivation to learn, I think it's difficult.

Also, a positive attitude toward the culture of the language to be learned is important. I think that if you're trying to learn a language and you have a negative image of the culture, of the country, of the society where that language is spoken, you may not be as motivated to learn. I believe that second language teachers should provide a stimulating and supportive atmosphere. I think they should provide a variety of activities in the classroom, it shouldn't just be group work, or just pair work, or just teacher-fronted lessons: there should be a variety of activities which are combined to create interest for the students and to take advantage of the lessons that you are teaching. Second languages should be taught creatively. They should take advantage of all the different methods and techniques available as much as possible. They should be taught with the learner in mind, and you should always keep in mind your own experiences as a learner. Try to put yourself in the place of the students. Try to think about how they're going to see this activity. What is important to explain to them, are they going to understand that this is an important or a useful activity? What are they going to get out of this activity? Is this going to be something they will find scary? Think about their culture when you're designing activities.

---

2 *Based on your own as well as on Ken's, Anne's, or Elizabeth's beliefs about second language learning and teaching, consider the impact that teachers' beliefs have on how teachers reason about their teaching and what they say and do in the classroom.*

In your reflective journal:

A. What are characteristics common to Ken's, Anne's, and Elizabeth's beliefs about second language learning and teaching? In what ways are your beliefs about second language learning and teaching similar to or different from these teachers'? Why do you think this is so?

With other teachers:

B. What might you expect to see if you walked into Ken's, Anne's, or Elizabeth's classroom? Can you anticipate what sort of teacher each would be based on his or her beliefs about second language learning and teaching?

CONFLICTING BELIEFS ABOUT LANGUAGE LEARNING AND TEACHING

If beliefs are grounded in episodic memories from prior experiences, then the language learning experiences of teachers will certainly have a powerful impact on their beliefs. This in itself can create conflicting beliefs for teachers because language learning does not always occur in the classroom. Informal language learning experiences in which the language functions as a means of meaningful communication in real social situations can leave powerful imprints on teachers because these sorts of informal language learning experiences tend to be vastly different from those that occur in the classroom. In fact, such conflicting language learning experiences can create havoc for teachers as they began to teach, because in most cases, their informal language learning experiences tend to be more positive, more meaningful, and more in line with the idealized image they hold for themselves as teachers. However, since these experiences occur outside the classroom, teachers may have few concrete models of how to recreate such experiences for their own students in their own classrooms. Moreover, the artificial nature of the language classroom itself makes most classroom activities pale in comparison to the experience of using language for meaningful communication, and both teachers and students know this.

SANDRA: BREAKING THROUGH THE LANGUAGE WALL

I've realized that the "me" who is a second language teacher is inextricably connected with the "me" who has struggled as a second language learner. I studied Spanish for two and a half years at my undergraduate university but I made little actual progress until I spent a semester in Spain. Fortunately, I did have mostly native speakers for professors at my school; unfortunately, most of them taught with a focus on grammar and a certain lack of interest in having us communicate in the classroom. I earned As with minimal work or investment. I regret that now, but at the time, almost all of my other classes were more demanding than Spanish and needed more deliberate attention. After all, how long does it really take for a good memorizer to prepare for a fill-in-the-blank exam every few weeks? Much less time than it takes for that same student to prepare for essay exams in literature classes, I realized very soon into my freshman year.

At any rate, the one communicative class I had was in my fifth semester: a Spanish literature course. The professor, an intimidating woman from Bogota, liked me because I actually made my stumbling way through all the assigned stories, unlike the other students in the class. I understood what the literature was about, and she could tell that. However, I could articulate very little about anything, and she knew that too. She called on me just as often as she called on the others in the class who were more able to speak, but after waiting a few moments, she would take pity on me and move on. I was thankful for that then, but when I got to Spain, I wished she had allowed me/forced me to talk in class.

My time in Spain was a semester of struggle; I was unprepared and intimidated. The courses I enjoyed most were those taught in Spanish with a focus on content—a course on contemporary Spanish history, and one on the politics, geography, economy, sociology, and the culture of Spain—because I could actually use the language for something, instead of being frustrated by focusing solely on the language. Those courses were more difficult than my composition, grammar, and conversation classes, but infinitely more satisfying.

One of the biggest frustrations for me in Spain was the feeling that I was kept from being myself by my weaknesses with Spanish. I hadn't realized this problem when I was conjugating verbs in my workbooks at my undergraduate university. It was only when Spanish became the only means of communication that I recognized how completely language can form a wall between people. I know who I am in English: I have a good idea of how intelligent I am, how curious I am, and what kind of sense of humor I have. But in Spanish, I turned into a person with seemingly little intelligence, curiosity only about the present (due to lack of mastery of complex past tense verbs), and no coherent sense of humor. I remember wanting to tell people, "Look, there's more to me than I'll ever be able to express in Spanish . . . Please believe me!"

The times that let me bring the real me out were the most satisfying learning times outside of class. I have vivid memories of sitting with my host mother Rosa, discussing what life was like when Franco was in control and how difficult the transition from that period had been. At that point, I could be intelligent and curious and interested in complicated and important things. And one of the best parts about improving my communicative ability was the increased opportunity to joke and laugh with one of my host brothers, Luis. Rosa and Luis were the only people who took the time and energy to talk to me and see who I might be if I could communicate well . . . and they were the only ones I was truly sad to leave. Their ability to look past the wall of the language was what encouraged me to learn and practice and care about communicating in Spanish at all.

When it became time for me to make the transition from language student to language student teacher, I spent half a semester in a high school Spanish classroom. My supervising teacher had lived in Mexico and was extremely proficient in Spanish. However, it seemed that the language was so easy for her that she had little patience for anyone—including her students—who struggled with it. From what I could tell, she saw the students as faulty language learners, not as language users or real people behind their fumbling verbs and mixed-up pronouns. Consequently, they were intimidated by her and her tendency to lose her temper unexpectedly at rambunctious behavior or language mistakes.

My favorite class, an eighth-period section that had only eight freshman students, was terrified of her. They lagged behind equivalent sections of Spanish because they had trouble understanding the grammar, and they frustrated her. I, on the other hand, identified with them largely because of my recent experiences in Spain, and we got along exceptionally well. I enjoyed getting to know them as people, and I tried to encourage them as beginning Spanish speakers. At that point in the spring, though, they were all planning to either quit Spanish forever or to sign up for a different teacher the next year. It was a matter of fear for them, not a matter of communication.

As a teacher now, I sometimes feel I've gone to an extreme because of these experiences, to the point where I focus on the learners and their ideas so much that I forget to work explicitly on the language. I concentrate on convincing students that they have real things to say and not worrying about how they say it until we've acknowledged and discussed the ideas. The problem with this approach is that sometimes we get so caught up in acknowledging and discussing that we never get to the language part. Nevertheless, I believe the trade-off is worth it. My interest in critical inquiry, in encouraging students to take a questioning stance . . . all that critical pedagogy "stuff" is founded on my goal of teaching individual people, not just learners with similar grammar errors.

Some of my favorite experiences as a teacher have been conferences in my office when students realize that I really wanted to know what they thought. This has happened when shy students admitted their homesickness to me, or when critical students finally recognized that I was interested in hearing their ideas, whether I agreed with them or not. At moments like those, they poke a few holes in the language barrier, and they can communicate as the people they are inside. They have a look I recognize (a look I was so happy to be able to use in Spain), a look that acknowledges and expresses gratitude for the time and energy required to put holes in the language barrier.

My goals for my students are related to who I am as a language learner. My natural tendency—as a language learner and a human being in general—is to resist those people who don't give me opportunities to be what I am. I am more receptive to those who patiently allow me to be me. For instance, the Spanish professors in Spain who viewed us as doers of worksheets, reciters of words, or givers of single-word answers never figured out who we were as people.

But the people who had me present and comment on news stories, synthesize information on essay tests, or tell my day's events over dinner showed that they saw me as an individual. They were more willing to accept my strengths, weaknesses, failed attempts, and unique successes. With them, I was a real person—a person capable of making decisions, making mistakes, and making my own way through the language learning wall.

RESOLVING CONFLICTING BELIEFS ABOUT LANGUAGE LEARNING AND TEACHING

Many language teachers are adamant about not recreating the same sorts of formal language learning experiences they had with their own teachers. Like Sandra, they strive to recreate their own informal language learning experiences inside the classroom. However, they often lack concrete models of how to do so, or if they are successful at recreating such experiences, as Sandra did with her students, they feel guilty about not "teaching" the language. This was evident in Sandra's comment, "I focus on the learners and their ideas so much that I forget to work explicitly on the language." Clearly, Sandra's image of a language teacher is someone who works explicitly on the language; an image that is grounded in her experiences in formal language classrooms.

So how can teachers resolve these conflicting beliefs in their own reasoning and teaching? In some ways they can't, at least not completely. The classroom will always be a classroom; "a place" according to Packer and Winne that is already "interpreted and understood; designed and produced to support and sustain a particular mode of teaching-and-learning" (1995, p. 2). For Sandra, these conflicting beliefs remain sources of conflict in both how she views herself as a teacher and how she reasons about her own teaching. She feels compelled to be that teacher who "teaches the language" while at the same time is driven by an inner desire to recreate language learning experiences for her students that allow them to express who they are and what they know. Sandra answers this question when she says, "I've realized that the 'me' who is a second language teacher is inextricably connected with the 'me' who has struggled as a second language learner."

But teachers can use their experiences of being a language learner to better understand how their students are experiencing their classroom practices. A former graduate student of mine recalled that she had never realized how anxiety-provoking a language classroom could be until she signed up for a conversational Japanese course. She admitted knowing nothing about Japanese when she enrolled in the course so she vividly recalled how her palms would sweat, her voice would crack, and her heart would race every time the teacher called on her. She claimed that this experience made her much more understanding of and sympathetic toward her students' affective needs, and to this day, she is always on the lookout for sweaty palms or cracking voices.

For many language teachers, their beliefs about themselves as teachers and their perceptions of their own instructional practices are influenced by images from their prior experiences in formal language classrooms. Such images represent the foundation for their epistemic beliefs—that is, beliefs they were not consciously aware of but that, like intuitive screens, colored their perceptions, thoughts, and actions in the classroom. Their epistemic beliefs are so strong that even though teachers are aware of the inadequacy of their beliefs and hold projected images of themselves as teachers that directly conflicted with these beliefs, they often feel powerless to alter their instructional practices because they have had few, if any, alternative images of teachers and teaching on which to base their classroom practices. Pajares claims that "the earlier a belief is incorporated into the belief structure, the more difficult it is to alter, for these beliefs subsequently affect perception and strongly influence the processing of information. It is for this reason that newly acquired beliefs are most vulnerable" (1992, p. 317). Thus teachers may experience a great deal of dissonance when they find themselves teaching in ways that are inconsistent with their projected or newly emerging beliefs about themselves as teachers and their teaching.

---

3 *REFLECTING ON CONFLICTING LANGUAGE LEARNING EXPERIENCES*

The following Investigations ask you to both recognize and reconcile conflicting language learning experiences that you may have had and to reflect on how these experiences shaped your knowledge about teaching.

In your reflective journal:

A. Reflect on your own experiences as a second language learner in both informal settings and formal second/foreign language classrooms. What was most memorable about these experiences and why?

B. Read Anne's and Elizabeth's accounts of their formal and informal language learning experiences below. How are their experiences different from each other's? How are their experiences different from or similar to your own language learning experiences? How do you think these experiences shape the kinds of teachers Anne and Elizabeth are today? How have your language learning experiences shaped the kind of teacher you are today?

Anne: I Just Felt Stupid at This Subject

My only classroom second language experiences took place in high school, and I was not successful at learning other languages. Therefore, I didn't want to pursue it. Now I'm sorry about that, but my experience . . . I took French for three years. The French teacher was excellent, as far as content, but she constantly made me repeat the sounds because I had a great deal of trouble pronouncing French words correctly, and I couldn't do it. I just couldn't do it, and it was the whole class watching me repeat these sounds. And the other thing that I noticed was there were some people who were very quick, could call out the answer before I had a chance to get it. And so I just felt stupid at this subject, and didn't want to pursue it. I could read it and write it fine, but as for speaking it, I just knew I could never learn to do that, so I didn't want to pursue it.

Another memorable second language learning experience was when I was a student in the education abroad program in France. At that time I went to France with about ten years of language learning behind me, ten years of French. And I remember when I first landed in France, I couldn't understand anything. They were speaking some language I had never heard before. And it was very difficult to make myself understood, and so I had to work really hard, but I was determined that I was going to fit in, that I was going to be able to communicate with the people and that I wouldn't be rebuffed because I wasn't speaking French perfectly or correctly. So, I hung around with French people, I had a French roommate. And I tried to really speak only French, even though there were other American students there, I just decided that I couldn't hang around with them because we would end up speaking English. So, by the end of the year, my speaking, listening, and reading were pretty good, because I was taking courses in French, regular university courses which were taught in French.

With other teachers:

B. Describe how your language learning experiences are different from or similar to Anne's, Elizabeth's, and/or Sandra's. Why do you think this is so? How have your own experiences as a second language learner in informal settings and/or formal second/foreign language classrooms shaped the type of language teacher you are today?

MANAGING CONFLICTING BELIEFS

If teachers' epistemic beliefs are to be refined, expanded, or transformed, and teachers' projected or newly emerging beliefs are to become more dominant, teachers must become cognizant of their own beliefs; question those beliefs in light of what they intellectually know and not simply what they intuitively feel; resolve conflicting images within their own belief systems; and have access to, develop an understanding of, and have successful encounters with alternative images of teachers and teaching.

SANDRA: THE TEACHER I WANT TO BE

On the Friday before Easter, my students were going to do office hour role plays and discuss their presentation topics. I had also planned on explaining the Easter Bunny during the last five minutes of class, because one of the students said his daughter had asked him about the Easter Bunny. When I left the class, however, we hadn't even looked at the role-play situations, and I still had no idea what they were planning on presenting. What we had done was discuss Easter, the Easter Bunny, atheism, Christianity, agnosticism, materialism, objectivism, subjectivism, idealism, deism, the tooth fairy, the big bang theory, and cough drops (there were connections between all of these things, though they may not be obvious at first glance). We'd done some monitoring (of their pronunciation problems), discussed word stress, and looked at new words that came up, but I knew that I hadn't pushed them to focus on their pronunciation problems as much as they could have.

We also hadn't related what we talked about to teaching, office hour interactions, or presentation skills. On the other hand, each of the eight students had been involved in the discussion, contributing his (they happen to be all male) knowledge about philosophy, religion, and logic. They were in control of the discussion and they were engaged, eager to provide and argue about information. I think that we each left slightly mentally exhausted, but aware that we'd discussed—and learned—something real. And even more importantly, each student in the class had been able to be himself: intelligent, knowledgeable, and capable of discussing subjects of real consequence.

This class, though not as typical as I'd like, represents the kind of class I know that I can teach when I'm being the teacher I want to be. It certainly had drawbacks: we neglected skills to work on ideas. But deep down in my teaching intuition, I believe that what happened in that classroom—academically and personally—is what language learning is all about.

I believe that learning a language is a process of gathering tools to use in expressing thoughts, ideas, and ourselves. These tools are essential for the processes of putting holes in the language barrier, of convincing people who cannot understand you that you are an individual different from the others around you, capable of thinking and worth knowing. In those processes, a teacher is a resource, a potential-recognizer, a guide who can show learners how to get where they want to go and break down the barriers in the way. Of course, it's the learners who decide what they want out of learning; they are active participants in the teaching/learning process, taking in the tools that seem useful and discarding or ignoring those that aren't. Teachers and learners all deal with the barrier of the language being learned, just as they deal with the goals, expectations, assumptions, and emotions that go along with teaching and learning a language.

My beliefs about language learning shape what happens in my classroom, and they create dimensions in my teaching that have both positive and negative sides. The things that I recognize as good in my teaching are based on my theories of language learning, learning in general, and critical pedagogy. The things that I recognize as flawed in my teaching come from my struggles to use those theories in ways that are effective and appropriate for my students in different contexts.

The positive side of my beliefs is that I am convinced that thinking is more important than grammar or pronunciation, and I believe students leave my class with more than just a few clearer target sounds or the ability to write a thesis statement. The dark side is that if I don't monitor myself, I concentrate on ideas and critical thinking to the exclusion of monitoring for pronunciation or correct verb tense. This is something I remind myself of often; it is another area where I need balance. My biggest fear is that my goals for the classroom and learning will conflict with students' expectations and they will be dissatisfied with the focus of the class. They, after all, are the ones learning the language, and they have to deal with it on a daily basis. I am afraid of not preparing them to face whatever waits for them outside of my classroom.

4 *REFLECTING ON WAYS OF MANAGING CONFLICTING BELIEFS*

Use this Investigation to explore how your own language learning experiences have come to shape your beliefs about language learning and teaching and the ways in which you manage the conflicting beliefs that you may hold.

In your reflective journal:

A. Why do you think Sandra worries about her belief that focusing on meaning is more important than focusing on form in second language teaching? How might she manage this conflict? Do you struggle with these conflicting beliefs about meaning versus form? How have you managed this conflict?

B. Describe the ways in which your beliefs about second language learning and teaching tacitly appear in your classroom practices

5 *EXPLORING COMMONLY HELD BELIEFS ABOUT TEACHERS AND TEACHING*

All of us have heard the comment "Teachers are born, not made." But why do people hold such conceptions of teachers and teaching? And how do such conceptions influence the beliefs that teachers hold when they enter the teaching profession? This Investigation will enable you to answer these questions and see their relevance for your own teaching.

Read the following statements:

Teachers teach the way they were taught.

There is a "right"way and a "wrong" way to teach.

Teachers learn to teach by teaching.

More experienced teachers are better teachers.

Teachers are born, not made.

A. In writing, reflect on each of these statements and state why you agree or disagree with each. Speculate on why people tend to believe these statements.

B. In a group, discuss why you agree or disagree with each statement. Speculate on why people tend to believe these statements.

C. In writing, reflect on your group discussion. Take note of one new insight you learned from your discussion. Describe how this new insight helped to broaden your conception of teachers and teaching.

Suggested Readings

Since much of the research on teachers' beliefs has struggled to define beliefs as a construct, I suggest starting with Robert Abelson's overview of the seven features that differentiate belief systems from knowledge systems in his article "Differences Between Belief and Knowledge Systems" (*Cognitive Science* 3: 355–366, 1979). For a rather academic but interesting overview of the research that has been carried out in general education on teachers' beliefs, I recommend M. Frank Pajares' 1992 article "Teachers' Beliefs and Educational Research: Cleaning Up a Messy Construct" (*Review of Educational Research* 62 (3): 307–332). Finally, Jan Nespor's 1987 article, "The Role of Beliefs in the Practice of Teaching" (*Curriculum Studies* 19: 317–328) and my own 1994 article "The Emerging Beliefs and Instructional Practices of Preservice ESL Teachers" (*Teaching and Teacher Education* 10 (4): 439–452) explore the role that teachers' beliefs play in teachers' conceptions of themselves, their teaching, and their learning to teach experiences.

Of course, the impact that teachers' beliefs have on their classroom practices are embedded in the stories teachers tell about their own professional lives. bell hooks' schooling experiences in rural all-black schools in the American South, described in *Teaching to transgress: Education as the practice of freedom* (New York: Routledge, 1994), instilled in her a belief that education was enabling, liberating, and would lead to freedom; beliefs that continue to permeate her teaching to this day. Stephen Brookfield's belief in the importance of questioning his own assumptions and beliefs about teachers, students, colleagues, and theory in *Becoming a critically reflective teacher* (San Francisco, CA: Jossey-Bass, 1995) form the foundation of his attempts to create a truly student-centered classroom. And finally, Pablo Freire's experiences as a college student working in literacy programs for peasants in Northern Brazil made him aware of the economic, social, and cultural oppression of the traditional educational system and were the impetus for the beliefs that ground his famous book *Pedagogy of the oppressed* (New York: Continuum, 1970).

4

LEARNING TO TEACH: BECOMING A LANGUAGE TEACHER

How do teachers learn to teach? Most people would say by teaching; so would most teachers. Given the power of teachers' apprenticeship of observation and the epistemic beliefs that emerge from their experiences both inside and outside classrooms, teachers' knowledge and beliefs have a tremendous impact on how teachers view themselves as teachers, what they learn from their professional course work, how they reason about their teaching, and how and why they teach the way they do. And while learning to teach is clearly much more than simply reconstructing in practice teachers' own images of teachers and teaching, it seems obvious that learning to teach does not occur solely within the venue of a teacher education program.

Learning to teach requires the acquisition of knowledge about all facets of classroom life. The complex developmental process of learning to teach occurs as a result of using your knowledge and beliefs to make sense of yourself as a teacher, your own teaching practices, your students, the content you are expected to teach, and the classroom and school within which you work. Such sense making is continually constructed and reconstructed within and out of your experiences, whether they be as a learner, as a teacher, or as a student of teaching in your professional development program. Richard's and Kate's experiences reflect this.

RICHARD: BAPTISM BY FIRE

Like most teachers, I can point to three primary areas of influence that have shaped me as a teacher—my own experience as a student, the students I have worked with as a teacher, and my teacher training. My experience as a student provided the foundations of my beliefs about learning and about the academic and moral responsibilities of teaching. My own students have helped me to expand and refine these beliefs. Without a doubt, I have learned the most about teaching from my students. My teacher training experience has had the least impact on my teaching, primarily because I have had comparatively little of it. Unlike most teachers, I do not have a degree in education. Not yet. I firmly believe that experience is the best teacher.

Throughout most of my elementary school years, I was considered a good student. Good meant that I always put forth my best effort and performed well on whatever it was that the teacher had required the class to do. Effort, performance, and success were specified and very rigidly controlled by the authority figure of the teacher. I performed according to the teacher's specifications so well, and was rewarded for doing so, that I suppose I was considered the teacher's pet more than once. My fifth/sixth-grade teacher entrusted me with the duty of carrying his bagged lunch downstairs to the refrigerator every morning and picking it up right before the class went to lunch. I never once broke his trust and looked inside that bag. Two years of carrying the man's lunch, and I have no idea what he ate.

From these experiences, I developed a clear sense that it is every teacher's responsibility to ensure that each individual student is made to feel important and worthy of the teacher's attention. I know I enjoyed my fifth/sixth-grade teacher's attention, but I have to wonder how his treatment of me affected the other students in the class. As a teacher, I want every one of my students to feel that he or she is important and has something valuable to contribute. I'm sure I don't always achieve this, and sometimes I really have to force myself to aim to achieve it for a particular student I just don't like (there's always one in the bunch), but I hold making each student feel important as an individual human being as one of my fundamental goals of a teacher.

I was always a shy kid. Being a teenager is confusing and awkward enough in our society for most kids. I think it is particularly tough on shy kids. At the age of sixteen, I found that alcohol, drugs, and cigarettes enabled me to feel more comfortable with myself, talk more freely, make friends, and just have fun. I had found my panacea. At the same time, I began listening to music that my father hated, questioning the validity of the religion on which I had been raised, trying to define myself as an individual distinct from the adults around me. I now see that I was not an atypical teenager. And despite what the adults said, I could do all this and still maintain an A-average in my classes.

But I suppose I had broken too many of the rules of the game. When the teachers at my high school met to nominate graduating seniors to the National Honor Society, they decided I was lacking in the moral qualifications necessary. I graduated second in a class of one hundred. I was the only one of the four speakers at commencement not wearing a National Honor Society ribbon.

Of course, I didn't really care about being a member of the National Honor Society. What affected me was the shame I was made to feel. Having received precious little guidance from any of the adults around me as to how to cope with the changes I was going through as a teenager and as to how to discover the adult human being I was becoming, I decided to do things my own way. The lack of comprehension exhibited, and the resultant fear felt and discrimination practiced by all those adults, who should have known better, stun me to this day.

I never allow value judgments to cloud my perspective as a teacher. As a human being, I might make value judgments about a student. But I feel it is my responsibility to allow and to encourage each student to develop as an individual, unfettered by my personal judgment of the goodness or rightness of who that individual is. I can't always extricate my values from my teaching, but I certainly can avoid imposing them on my students. To be made to feel ashamed for not playing by someone else's rules, for trying to discover the world on one's own without causing any harm to anyone else, is something to which I would never subject a fellow human being.

After five or six weeks of intensive training in Peace Corps English as a foreign language teaching methodology, I was shipped off to my little Chadian town on the edge of the Sahara and given three classes to teach. I like to refer to the experience as baptism by fire. For most of that first year, I stood in front of my classes and told them about English. I made the students pronounce words and sometimes attempt sentences, but I don't think there was too much communication going on in English. My second year in the Peace Corps, I was posted in another town. I was given the task of teaching beginning EFL to five classes of seventh-grade students. There were eighty or so students in each class. I didn't give too many written assignments that year.

By the second year, my teaching style did change drastically. Every one of my students was proficient in two, sometimes three, languages. They needed to teach me about language learning. But perhaps the greatest force behind the change was the knowledge that I had studied French for four years in high school through a grammar-translation method and, though I certainly appreciated my French teacher as a human being, I only really learned French as I was having to use it in Chad to communicate.

Despite the number of students I taught my second year in the Peace Corps, my sense of the student as an individual was further refined. In Chad, a minority of children are allowed by their families to continue schooling after the elementary grades. Having made it to high school, the value of education was particularly significant to these kids. I watched as Chadian teachers, not unlike many American teachers I've seen, set students up for failure. I've never understood the motivation for that. My responsibility to set up my students—each individual—for success became apparent.

Upon returning to the United States, I worked for several months teaching ESL to adults in the Washington, D.C., area. Then I secured a position as a special education teacher in a public school in Maryland. The idea of working with kids who needed special consideration appealed to me. How rewarding such work would be.

Not! I was a young, white, idealistic teacher, fresh from teaching in a country where students respected the authority of the teacher no matter what, coming to a tough cynical, all-black school, where the students' first priority was to challenge the authority and credibility of the teacher. The district's answer to mainstreaming of special education students was to lump all the special education students into one class and then assign a special education teacher to follow that class around throughout the five periods with content-area teachers. My position, then, was keeper of the sixth-grade special education class at my school.

For most of that year, I felt like I did battle with those kids. They resented my presence since I was a constant reminder that they had been labeled as different, as somehow not normal. They, understandably, took their anger out on me. In addition, they were well aware of the fact that I was incapable of talking or being like them and they took advantage of that. I, on the other hand, was determined to communicate with them as a teacher in a way that I felt they as students needed to learn. As a new teacher in this district, I had gone through an orientation in which I was told that African-American children needed hands-on learning and I needed to be aware of this different learning style. My kids did have very different learning styles, but their being African-American in and of itself had little to do with it. I saw a clear need to avoid such generalizations because, no matter how well-intentioned, I felt they led to lowered expectations.

I held high expectations for each of those students as individuals, with individual learning styles, individual learning needs, and individual strengths and weaknesses. By the end of the school year I had learned ways to more effectively bridge the differences between me and the students and to present my expectations to them in a more positive way. But I've never for a minute regretted holding those kids to a standard that the system, and the kids themselves, initially told me they were incapable of achieving. Although I experienced the worst burnout of my teaching career during that year, I'll never forget the good-bye card they gave me at the end of the school year. Each wrote something very short, but sweet, and one student, who was something of a leader in the class and with whom I had fought tooth and nail all year, signed it "Love, Your Friend." I was most touched.

In my next job, I again encountered a system that I felt was miserably failing the children entrusted to its care. I worked for three years in a special program funded by the Department of Education to develop and implement an ESL program for limited English proficiency students who had been identified as exhibiting some type of disability. The program operated in two schools. One was an elementary school for visually impaired children. Thanks in large part to a strong principal, that school was a model of effective instruction. Sadly, it was a model of effective education in a sea of dysfunction. The high school in which the second program operated was more typical of the dysfunction endemic to the district. The high school was a massive, intimidating five-story building in which about three thousand kids were supposedly receiving an education.

The principal was an alcoholic. Many of the teachers and other staff had burnt out long ago. On any given day, approximately half the student population was absent and there was a good chance that quite a few of those who were present were carrying a weapon.

And then there were our kids—impaired by unpleasant or traumatic experiences as refugees, by limited English proficiency, by learning difficulties, by the dysfunctional system assigned to educate them, and by poverty. But I saw in those kids something that I saw in the students I had worked with in Chad: the essentially human ability of the individual to adjust to, and potentially overcome, whatever obstacles one encounters. These students were simply lacking in the skills needed to confront those obstacles, and the adults whose job it was to assist them in acquiring those skills were either incapable of doing so or they didn't care, or both.

It became very clear to me that I had a responsibility to empower my students by helping them to understand their world and by assisting them to acquire the skills needed to engage that world and to make that world, no matter how dysfunctional, respond to their needs. I was a critical pedagogist before reading Freire or Giroux. Our primary goal, then, was to help my students develop the conceptual knowledge they needed to make sense of their world. The English language was the vehicle I used to teach that conceptual knowledge. I did a lot of advocating for these kids before they were able to use what they had learned to advocate for themselves. But that in itself served as a model that most of them began to emulate.

The courses I've taken in my teacher education program have caused me to rethink a lot of assumptions I had about ESL teaching and teaching in general. Mostly the program has effectively helped me to reexamine and refine aspects of my teaching that I had previously seen as adequate. Among other things, I'm reconsidering my perspectives on the place of grammar and pronunciation in the ESL classroom, on bilingual education and the importance of students' first languages and cultures, and on the discontinuities that can exist between teachers and minority students. I've also thought quite a bit about the patterns of communication that I establish in my classroom. Having worked primarily with kids, and in particular with kids I perceived as needing a lot of structure, I suppose I've been a bit more controlling in terms of what goes on in my classroom than I had thought myself to be. Taking this realization as a challenge, I decided to put more of the control into the hands of my students and was thrilled to find that my classroom didn't degenerate into anarchy as a result.

I believe I now teach in accordance with my beliefs about making each student feel important, allowing and encouraging each individual to express him- or herself, setting students up for success, holding high expectations, helping students understand and function in their worlds, and allowing them to have a lot more control over the direction of their learning.

KATE: THE KIND OF TEACHER I WANT TO BE

I guess I always knew I'd become a teacher. Both my parents were teachers. I have vivid memories of the two of them huddled around the kitchen table with milk crates overflowing with folders of student work that needed to be graded. There were always red pens in my house. I was the only one who brought in absentee excuses in red ink, my lunch bag had my name on it in red ink, my clothes labels were initialed in red ink. Red pens and being a teacher were synonymous in my mind. So were messy classrooms. I'd hang out in my father's classroom after school or on the weekends and it was always a mess. Not messy in the bad sense of the word, but messy from the remnants of activity: papers, books, boxes, pencils, crayons, glue, magazines, workbooks, posters, chalk, sticks, tacks, paints, lunchboxes, boots, mittens, hats, and on and on. While I waited for him to organize the piles of papers that always seemed to clutter his desk, I'd clean the chalkboard erasers, feed the classroom hamster, and poke around in the activity stations he had set up at the back of his classroom. The other thing I associated with teaching was noise. The few times I actually watched my father teach, the noise in his classroom was deafening. Everyone was doing something, everyone was talking, and when my father wanted his voice to be heard, he'd simply yell louder. "Don't forget to put your names on your papers!" he'd shout over the constant drone of noise.

When I finally went off to school I found that most of my classrooms were not at all like my father's. In second grade we had to keep our "cubbies" neat, we cleaned out our desks every Friday, and learning and teaching were confined to the chalkboard and what was in our textbooks. In sixth grade we sat in rows, boy-girl-boy-girl; we were expected to be quiet, orderly, and in control at all times. There were some exceptions, though. In fourth grade we sat around big tables, we could move around the room, there were always lots of books and magazines to look through, and we did things in groups. In junior and senior high school, most of the classrooms were pretty sterile places. That may have been because we moved from room to room throughout the day and so did most of our teachers. Teachers told us things, and we wrote them down and got tested on them later. Teachers asked us questions and we answered them. Teachers talked to us and we talked back to them. We read things in books and filled in the blanks in workbooks.

School wasn't much of an effort. I was a good student. I did what I was told. I got good grades. I hung out with the good kids. My parents were teachers in the district, so most of my teachers knew about me before I entered their classrooms. When they'd call attendance on the first day of school, they'd check me out as if to say, "Oh, so you're so-and-so's kid." If I got into trouble I knew my parents would find out about it before I got home, so I behaved. I played the game. Sometimes the game was fun; at other times I just went through the motions. In high school I liked English because we got to read "real" books and talk about them. Some books were better than others, but most of them took me to a world outside school.

When I declared my major in college, no one was surprised that it was elementary education. My mother seemed proud, while my father felt compelled to warn me that I'd work hard and not make much money, but that he knew I'd be a great teacher. My teacher education courses seem like a blur to me now. We read about kids and learning and teaching. We wrote sample lesson plans for no one, created fake teaching units for classes we would never teach, designed science projects that no one would ever conduct, and pretended to teach each other in mock simulations. We did get to go into a classroom or two now and then, but the teachers always seemed to be too busy to deal with us. Usually we got stuck at the back of the room helping the slower kids finish their workbook assignments, or we copied and collated papers for the teacher.

When it came time for me to do my student teaching I couldn't wait. This was my big chance to be the kind of teacher I wanted to be. I envisioned a class of fifth graders busily involved with hands-on activities, doing things, not just learning about things, talking to each other and learning together. I envisioned a messy, noisy room where kids would be excited about learning and I'd be excited about teaching. Boy, was I in for a shock! The desks were in rows; the posters on the bulletin board looked ancient, yellowed from their years of use; the teacher stood at the front of the room with the teacher's book in her hands; she asked questions and the students answered; it was quiet, controlled, and orderly. I was disappointed. But I could function in this classroom because I'd been in classrooms like this one before. In fact, I'd been successful in classrooms like this one. But I knew deep down inside that this wasn't the kind of teacher I wanted to be and this wasn't the kind of classroom I wanted to be in anymore.

After I spent a few weeks sitting at the back of the room or reading aloud to the lowest-level reading group, my cooperating teacher suggested that I teach the upcoming science unit on volcanoes. I jumped at the chance. Finally, I'd have a chance to teach and I could teach the way I wanted. I created this elaborate bulletin board display that illustrated a cross-section of a volcano. I dug up an old science kit that explained how kids could make volcanoes that actually erupted. I found a movie from the school's antiquated film collection on volcanoes. I went to the geology department on campus and got some samples of various types of volcanic rock and ash. I got as many books as I could find on volcanoes from the public library. Once I had all this "stuff" in my dorm room, I began to realize that I wasn't sure what I was going to do with it, so I called my father. He offered words of encouragement and a confident "You'll figure it out!" My cooperating teacher encouraged me to stick to the textbook for my first time around. My university supervisor suggested that I write out a lesson plan and then come talk to her. Panic began to set in.

Fortunately, there were two other student teachers in my school, and while sharing rides back and forth to campus, we started talking about my volcano unit. Neither of them offered much in the way of concrete ideas about how to teach this unit, but they were a great sounding board. I found that after talking through what I thought I wanted to do with them, I came to understand what I wanted to do for myself. I did write out a lesson plan, although I'm not sure if it really helped all that much, and I did use the textbook to sort of organize the overall unit.

I can't even recall what transpired as a result, except for the fact that it was messy and noisy; there were moments of chaos and others of true engagement and excitement. I discovered quickly that the students didn't know how to work in groups, they got carried away with all the activity and movement around the room, and I found myself asserting control over their behavior and the noise. I quickly learned you have to structure unstructured activities if you want students to know what to do and be able to do it on their own. I learned that you have to make the classroom a predictable place so students will know what is expected of them and can meet your expectations. I had to learn to think on my feet and when students gave me answers I wasn't expecting, I had to figure out some way to connect their ideas to what I was trying to teach them. I learned to balance freedom and control, neatness and messiness, and noise and quietness.

I also learned that I had a very different conception of what teaching was than the adults around me. I'll never forget the day my university supervisor came in to observe me teach and when she saw the students working busily at the work stations I had set up around the room, she whispered, "I'll come back when you're teaching." If this wasn't teaching, what was?

On a fluke, I ended up going to Mexico and found a job teaching EFL because I was a native speaker of English. It was an easy transition for me because a messy, noisy, lively EFL classroom worked great for children who wanted to learn English. I couldn't use a textbook because we didn't have one, so I used lots of American music, magazines, movies, and books, and we played a lot of games. They taught me games in Spanish and I taught them games in English. Anyway, you can't learn English in rows, in silence, out of a textbook. I should know—I took eight years of Spanish in such a classroom and could hardly communicate when I arrived in Mexico.

When I enrolled in graduate school to get a degree in TESOL I realized that what I had done with my Mexican EFL students and even with my fifth-grade students was theoretically sound. I had given them comprehensible input, I just didn't call it that. We used realia, I just didn't call it that. I used total physical response, I just didn't know it had a name. What I remember most from my graduate work is that I finally understood how my students were learning English and what I could do to enhance that learning experience for them. But I learned a lot about myself. I learned that it was OK to have a messy, noisy room; that if I had a purpose for what I was doing and the students knew what that purpose was, language learning and meaningful communication would occur in my classroom. When I think about the kind of teacher I am now, I realize that I haven't changed all that much. I use red pens a lot; my classrooms are always messy, but it's an organized mess; they are noisy, but it's productive, lively noise; I expect my students to do things with the language, not just learn about it; and I work long hours and don't make much money, but that's OK too. At least I'm the kind of teacher I want to be.

---

1 *REFLECTING ON LEARNING-TO-TEACH EXPERIENCES*

After reading about Richard's and Kate's learning-to-teach experiences, complete this Investigation to help you begin thinking about your own learning-to-teach experiences.

In your reflective journal:

Can you relate to the learning-to-teach experience of Richard or Kate? How are your experiences similar to or different from theirs? Why do you think this is so?

LEARNING TO TEACH

Many of the teachers with whom I work enter the classroom with idealized views about creating a learning environment that is interactive and communicative, only to find themselves obsessed with classroom control and discipline. They are surprised when their students don't respond in kind to an activity that they, as students, once found enjoyable. Their knowledge of classroom life tends to be limited to what they experienced as students and thus does not account for what they experience when they enter the classroom as the teacher. This dilemma is supported by recent research, which suggests that teachers learn about teaching through their prolonged apprenticeship of observation and that these experiences have a much greater impact on learning to teach than the content of or their experiences in any sort of teacher education program (Carter, 1990; Kagan, 1992).

As teachers learn to teach, they tend to progress through different stages of concern. Developmental models of learning to teach suggest that new teachers focus on mastering the procedural knowledge necessary to maintain classroom control and discipline before they are able to turn their attention to what they are teaching or to student learning (Berliner, 1986; Fuller, 1969). Kagan (1992) argues that this introspective viewpoint of new teachers may be beneficial since it enables them to adapt and reconstruct their idealized images of teachers and teaching so that they are more in tune with the realities of classroom life. As their procedural knowledge becomes more automated and they gain more knowledge about their students, they are better able to reconceptualize the content they are expected to teach from their students' perspective and can develop a repertoire of reasoned instructional considerations to inform their classroom practices.

While developmental models of learning to teach may argue that acquiring procedural knowledge in the form of standardized routines for dealing with classroom management is a necessary prerequisite if new teachers are to turn their attention toward positive student learning and effective instructional practices, Grossman (1992) counters that an early emphasis on procedural knowledge carries with it the implication that procedural knowledge is the most important aspect of learning to teach and, thus, that new teachers may focus on little else. Instead, she argues that new teachers can and do reflect deeply on issues related to the intellectual and moral aspects of teaching and therefore must be encouraged to "struggle simultaneously with issues of management, social roles and routines in classrooms, instruction, and learning" (p. 175).

New teachers need procedural knowledge about the day-to-day operations of managing and teaching. They need to see their students as individuals with unique needs, interests, aptitudes, and personalities. However, more importantly, they need to place this procedural knowledge and knowledge of students within the context of alternative models of teachers and teaching so as to avoid maintaining the status quo and, essentially, reproducing their own apprenticeship of observation. For many language teachers, their formal language learning experiences were vastly different from those they wish to create in their own classrooms. As Kate noted "you can't learn English in rows, in silence, out of a textbook. I should know—I took eight years of Spanish in such a classroom and could hardly communicate when I arrived in Mexico." But Kate had an alternative model of teachers and teaching—her parents, whose models of teaching left a lasting impression on what she believes is possible and appropriate in the classroom.

If learning to teach is effected mostly by our experiential knowledge as students, then what do teachers learn from their teacher education programs? Some would argue, not much; that typically teachers exit their teacher education programs with the same set of knowledge and beliefs about teachers, students, teaching, and learning they had when they entered, assuming that what they do not know, they will learn on the job. Kagan places the blame squarely on teacher education programs for

> failing to provide novices with adequate procedural knowledge of classrooms, adequate knowledge of pupils or the extended practica needed to acquire that knowledge, or a realistic view of teaching in its full classroom/school context. (1992, p. 162)

In addition, she argues that theoretical course work offered at the university tends to be highly irrelevant when it comes to coping with the demands of actual classroom practice. Most teacher education programs, she chides, fail to recognize what things teachers bring to the program that shape how and what they learn there. Therefore, the knowledge that new teachers do acquire in their teacher education programs remains vastly different from the way teachers actually use their knowledge in the classroom. Kate's complaint sums up Kagan's concerns succinctly: "We wrote sample lesson plans for no one, created fake teaching units for classes we would never teach, designed science projects that no one would ever conduct, and pretended to teach each other in mock simulations."

Despite the criticisms levied against teacher education programs, some take a more optimistic view of the role that such programs play in the process of learning to teach. Freeman (1991) conducted an eighteen-month longitudinal study in which he reported on how foreign language teachers' conceptions of their classroom practice developed as they took part in an in-service teacher education program. At the outset of the study, Freeman characterized these teacher conceptions of their practice as embracing a series of tensions between fostering real world language use over more artificial classroom language, balancing spontaneous interaction over maintaining control over classroom discipline, and viewing students as individuals rather than a collective group in the language learning process. Freeman also found that these teachers drew on two main sources to both express and rationalize these tensions. These included the norms of their own schooling experiences, which reflected a teacher-centered conception of practice, and by their conception of teaching as a step-by-step process, influenced most by the central role of the textbook in carrying out foreign language instruction.

After following these teachers through two consecutive summer in-service experiences and the intervening year, Freeman found that these teachers began to develop a shared professional discourse that reflected the language of the in-service program, and thus developed new ways of coding or naming their understandings of teaching. As he described it:

> The shared professional discourse about teaching and learning
> which they have encountered and incorporated into their ways
> of thinking and acting as teachers helps them, in Shulman's words,
> "to make the tacit explicit." . . . It delineates a community which
> shares perceptions and values and it permits these teachers to refer
> to, and ultimately think of, themselves as members of that commu-
> nity. At the same time, it organizes their thinking about teaching by
> providing them with a means to articulate explanations and thus
> to construct understandings of their practice. (1991, p. 452)

Like Freeman, Yinger (1987) likens learning to teach to learning to think and act in ways appropriate to the demands of the teaching profession. In fact, Yinger characterizes the teaching profession as a culture, one in which the language represents the shared perceptions, conceptions, and acceptable actions of its members. Thus, "learning the language of practice" (p. 293) becomes central to learning to teach, since without knowledge of the language of practice, teachers cannot operate as full members of the culture of teaching. Kate found that the theoretical knowledge presented in her master's in TESOL program gave her a way of renaming her classroom practices, giving what she intuitively thought of as appropriate for her students a theoretical justification.

Proponents of teacher education programs argue that the systematic knowledge and reflective experiences of professional development activities create invaluable opportunities for teachers to question their beliefs and assumptions about teachers, students, learning, and teaching; to reexamine the subject matter they are teaching from a purely pedagogical vantage point and develop sound explanations for their classroom practices; to explore the theoretical foundations and pedagogical and social implications of their classroom practices; and to critically reflect, in a deliberate and detailed way, on the connections between the knowledge, beliefs, and criteria that guide their classroom practices. Without time, opportunity, and support for these sorts of professional development experiences, new teachers are susceptible to narrowly defined conceptions of who teachers are, what teaching is, who their students are, how students learn, and the subject matter they are expected to teach. As Richard found "the [teacher education] program has effectively helped me to reexamine and refine aspects of my teaching that I had previously seen as adequate."

No one learns to teach solely as a result of a teacher education program, but such programs can create opportunities for teachers to come to understand who they are by recognizing their beliefs about themselves as teachers, and about teaching and learning in language classrooms. They can enable teachers to come to understand who their students are by recognizing their strengths and weaknesses as learners, their preferences as people, and their expectations and assumptions about classrooms and schools. They can create opportunities for teachers to make sense of what they do by reflecting on their own instructional practices so as to come to terms with inconsistencies between what they want to do during instruction and what actually happens. They can enable teachers to recognize how classrooms work. Moreover, they can foster discussions about the broader social, cultural, and political ramifications of language teaching and learning, particularly issues related to enculturation and assimilation into dominant English-speaking societies, often at the expense of second language students' own cultural identities (Gee, 1988).

Learning to teach is not a singular event, with a start and a finish. It is not limited to a particular place, with boundaries that confine its growth. Learning to teach is a long-term, complex, socially constructed, developmental process that is acquired by participating in the social practices associated with teaching and learning. It is affected by the sum of our experiences, some figuring more prominently than others. It requires the acquisition and interaction of knowledge and beliefs about oneself as a teacher, of the content to be taught, of one's students, and of classroom life. It is the combination of such experiences, knowledge, and beliefs, when situated in the context of real classrooms, that forms the foundation for teachers' reasoning and the justifications for their classroom practices.

---

2 *Constructing Learning-to-Teach Histories*

Learning-to-teach histories represent the experiences that mold the educational thinking of teachers and include the varied experiences that teachers bring with them to teacher education programs. Constructing a learning-to-teach history can help you better understand the experience of becoming a teacher and the impact that your life experiences have on your views of teaching and your teaching practices.

    A. Write a learning-to-teach history that explores how you came to your decision to become a teacher and what you hope to accomplish as a teacher. Identify important people or critical incidents that significantly influenced your understandings of teachers and teaching.

B. As you construct your learning-to-teach history, reflect on the most salient personal and professional experiences that have influenced your conceptions of yourself as a teacher and your understanding of your teaching practices.

C. Share your learning-to-teach history with a group of teachers and/or your instructor.

- Discuss the similarities and/or differences found among the learning-to-teach histories.

- Discuss what you learned from writing your learning-to-teach history.

- Discuss what you learned from hearing about others' learning-to-teach histories.

Suggested Readings

There are two very good academic reviews of the research on teacher learning from the general educational literature, one by Donna Kagan, "Professional Growth Among Preservice and Beginning Teachers" (*Review of Educational Research* 62 (2): 129–169, 1992) and the other by Kathy Carter, "Teachers' Knowledge and Learning to Teach" in *Handbook of research on teacher education* (New York: Macmillan, pp. 291–310, 1990). For an excellent account of learning to teach from a critical perspective, I recommend Deborah Britzman's book *Practice makes practice: A critical study of learning to teach* (Albany, NY: SUNY Press, 1991). From a teacher's perspective, both Sylvia Ashton-Warner's book *Teacher* (New York: Simon & Schuster, 1963) and Garret Keizer's book *No place but here: A teacher's vocation in a rural community* (New York: Viking Press, 1988) provide personal accounts of the trials and tribulations of learning to teach.

5

TEACHERS' REASONING
IN ACTION

To understand the complex nature of teachers' reasoning we must consider two fundamental questions: What do teachers think about as they teach and how do they think about these things? My answer to the first question is "a lot." My answer to the second question is "it depends."

Teachers think about all sorts of things as they teach. They think about their subject matter content and how they can sequence the presentation and manipulation of that content in order to reach the overall goals of their lessons. They think about their students, whether they understand what is going on during the lesson, whether they are motivated and involved in the lesson, what sort of language skills and abilities they have, and their social and affective needs as learners in their classrooms. They think about their own teaching; how to manage the time and the tasks; and how and when students will participate in those tasks. They continually judge the appropriateness of their own teaching strategies so as to balance the needs of their students with the goals of the lesson.

How teachers think about these things depends on a host of considerations, some grounded in teachers' experiential and professional knowledge and beliefs, others shaped by the professional landscapes in which the teachers live and work. How they think about their subject matter content depends on their own experiences as learners of that content, their understanding of how that content is viewed and organized within the discipline, and the theoretical orientation and instructional importance placed on the materials they use. How they think about their students depends on their own experiences as students; their beliefs about how students should act and learn; the academic, social, and personal expectations they hold for their students; and how their students are viewed within the context of the schools and within the surrounding communities in which they live. How they think about their own teaching depends on their own prior learning and teaching experiences; their conceptions of themselves as teachers; how they make sense of their own teaching; and the expectations they hold for themselves, their teaching, and for their students within their own classrooms.

Thus we begin our exploration into the complexities of teachers' reasoning by examining what teachers think about as they teach (teacher decision making) and by investigating how teachers think about these things within their own instructional contexts (teachers' interpretations). Of course, these two aspects of teachers' reasoning do not operate in isolation from one another; instead, they are interrelated and interdependent. However, both have emerged from an area of educational research known as "teacher cognition" that has focused on the complex conceptual processes of teachers teaching. By grounding our conceptualization of teachers' reasoning in this research, we will bring to the surface a view of teaching that is often hidden from public view—one that recognizes the complex, situated, interpretive, and dynamic cognitive processes that shape teachers' reasoning and, in turn, determine their teaching practices.

TEACHERS' DECISION MAKING

In the 1970s, a relatively large body of research began to emerge in mainstream teacher education that attempted to describe teachers' interactive thoughts, judgments, and decisions while teaching (Clark & Peterson, 1986; Shavelson & Stern, 1981). Teachers were thought to be rational people who made rational decisions about what to do in their classrooms based on rational principles of learning and teaching. Experienced teachers were found to possess a well-organized knowledge base regarding the students and the classroom environment that enabled them to simplify, differentiate, and transform information during instruction and also make alternative choices without disrupting the flow of instruction (Calderhead, 1981).

Much of teachers' decision making was characterized as reflecting well-established instructional routines (Clark & Peterson, 1986; Shavelson & Stern, 1981). That is, during instruction teachers relied on well-established routines, constantly monitoring the classroom to determine whether a routine should proceed as planned. If necessary, teachers might call up another routine developed from previous experience, or if no routine was available, they would react spontaneously and then continue teaching. This characterization meant that to reflect on an alternative decision drastically increased the cognitive demands placed on the teacher, and therefore, instructional routines would help minimize the amount of "cognitive overload" that teachers might experience during instruction. Shavelson wrote:

> Teachers' main concern during interactive teaching is to maintain the flow of the activity. To interrupt this sequence to reflect on an alternative and consider the possibility of changing a routine drastically increases the information-processing demands on the teacher and increases the probability of classroom management problems. (1983, p. 408)

It was also found that, unlike experienced teachers, novice teachers had not developed a schema for interpreting and coping with what goes on during instruction, nor did they possess a repertoire of instructional routines on which they could rely. Instead, novice teachers had to consciously make an overwhelming number of instructional decisions while teaching, and consequently tended to focus on disruptive student behavior and on maintaining the flow of activities (Fogarty, Wang, & Creek, 1983). At the time it was proposed that novice teachers be trained in effective instructional decision-making skills so they would be able to think like their more experienced colleagues.

My interest in this research on teacher decision making was fueled by my genuine concern for the preservice ESL teachers I was supervising during their practicum experience. I hoped that if I could understand what these teachers thought about as they taught, I would be able to get a better sense of the complex nature of their interactive decision making and, I hoped, would be better able to help them deal with the complexities of learning to teach. For fifteen weeks I explored the instructional decisions and actions of six preservice ESL teachers during their practicum teaching experience (see Johnson, 1992). I collected videotaped observations of their actual classroom instruction, stimulus recall reports of the instructional decisions they recalled making and the prior knowledge they recalled considering as they viewed their own videotaped instruction, and written retrospective accounts of what they perceived to have had the greatest influence on their decisions during their videotaped instruction. I wanted to determine the ways in which these teachers interpreted and responded to what their second language students said and did and to identify the instructional considerations and prior knowledge they considered when making specific instructional decisions.

The findings of my research identified eight different categories of instructional considerations that these teachers thought about as they taught.

Instructional consideration	Teacher recalls making a decision with consideration for	Description
Student motivation and involvement	the need to increase or maintain student motivation and involvement	Teachers often make certain instructional decisions or alter their instructional practices to increase and/or maintain their students' motivation and involvement in their lessons.
Instructional management	the effect of overall group process on the instructional flow of the lesson	To manage the instructional flow of any lesson, teachers must manage the time, the tasks, and how and when students participate in those tasks.
Curriculum integration	the sequence of the lesson content and/or instructional materials	While a single lesson may be made up of several instructional activities, teachers must consider how to sequence those activities so as to achieve the overall instructional goal of that lesson.
Student affective needs	students' social, affective, and developmental needs	Lowering second language students' affective filter is essential if students are to feel comfortable participating in a lesson.

Subject matter content	the nature of the lesson content	Ensuring that students learn the subject matter content and have an opportunity to use that content in meaningful ways is an important instructional consideration for teachers.
Student understanding	the need to increase or ensure student understanding	Teaching students who have limited English proficiency forces teachers to constantly judge whether those students understand what is going on during a lesson.
Student language skill and ability	the level of student language skill and ability	Teaching students who have limited English proficiency requires that teachers adjust their responses and their instructional activities to match the specific language skill and ability of their students.
Appropriateness of teaching strategy	the appropriateness of a particular teaching strategy	Teachers continually judge the appropriateness of a particular teaching strategy, and sometimes alter that teaching strategy to fit the needs of their students or the goals of the lesson.

While all eight categories of instructional considerations were used by these preservice ESL teachers, most of their decisions were made with consideration for ensuring student understanding, motivation, and involvement, as well as instructional management. At the same time, they continually questioned the appropriateness of their teaching strategies, appearing to judge their own effectiveness in relation to what their students said and did and, thereby, seeking confirmation throughout their lessons that their students understood and were actively engaged.

For example, in Excerpt 1 below, this teacher recalled deciding to encourage elicited responses as a means of maintaining student motivation and involvement, but perceived one student's continued initiations as interrupting the flow of the instructional activity. She then recalled questioning the appropriateness of her own teaching strategy, and therefore decided not to utilize the student's initiations, but instead to continue with the instructional activity as planned.

Excerpt 1

Instructional Action	Student Performance Cue	Instructional Decision	Prior Knowledge
T: What other sections of the newspaper do you like? *(Checks Knowledge)*	S1: Business. *(Elicited Response)*	I decided to ask them about the sections of the paper that they read so they might be more interested in the activity I had planned. *(Student Motivation & Involvement)*	
T: Business, what sort of information do you get there? *(Elicits & Incorporates Input)*	S1: Stocks. *(Elicited Response)*		
T: Interesting, so you like to read about stocks? *(Elicits & Incorporates Input)*	S1: Because I am a marketing major, and I always look in the same place in the newspaper, you open the newspaper and you look for the same thing, you only look at the same thing, it's like a custom. *(Initiation)*		
T: So you're accustomed to looking at that section? *(Elicits & Incorporates Input)* T: O.K.	S1: For my class, yes, economics, I look everyday and I get informations that I bring to class and all the students talk about it in my class. *(Initiation)*		She was off topic here and so was I. I need to stay on topic. *(Appropriateness of Teaching Strategy)*
T: O.K. How about [S2], what sections of the newspaper do you read? *(Checks knowledge)*	S1: I know a lot about this, but my friends say, you crazy, they read comic but I read stocks. *(Initiation)*		I decided to ask the others so we could get on with the activity. *(Instructional Management)*

Johnson, 1992, p. 520

Some other very interesting patterns of teacher thinking also emerged. I found that these teachers paid more attention to errors and deficient responses by implementing a cycle of instructional actions that included checking knowledge, providing an explanation, and giving feedback. They paid less attention to elicited and initiated responses by either eliciting and incorporating student initiations or giving feedback. When faced with unexpected student responses such as deficient responses, continued student initiations, or errors, these teachers relied on a limited number of instructional actions and often perceived such responses as obstacles to maintaining control over the instructional activities. When students produced incorrect, insufficient, or superfluous responses, teachers tended to check student knowledge, provide an explanation, and give feedback.

Excerpt 2

Instructional action	Student performance cue	Instructional decision	Prior knowledge
T: What kind of time are we talking about here? (Checks Knowledge)	S1: Happening now. (Error)		We had been over this before, so I expected him to know this. (Student Skill, Ability, & Knowledge)
T: No, we don't know if it is raining right now. (Gives Feedback) Is it happening right now? (Checks Knowledge)	S1: Yes. (Error)		
T: No, it's not raining now. (Gives Feedback) It has been raining all morning, so we are saying that it rained all morning, but we don't know if it is raining now, it might have stopped. (Explains Concept/ Procedure) It has been raining all morning, so what time are we talking about? (Checks Knowledge)	S1: Past (Error)	He clearly didn't understand this so I decided to go over the whole thing again. (Student Understanding) I thought, "Well, I'll try one more time," because I still wasn't sure if he understood it or not. (Student Understanding)	

T: Well, you're right
it started in the past.
(Gives Feedback)
But it started raining
in the past and it
came up to the
present, but we don't
know if it is raining
right now.
*(Explains Concept/
Procedure)*

I'm frustrated
here because my
explanations aren't
getting through to
him and I don't know
what else I can do
to make it clearer.
*(Appropriateness of
Teaching Strategy)*

T: Look at number 3.
*(Focuses Attention/
Effort)*

I decided to move
on, because he
was holding up
the entire lesson.
*(Instructional
Management)*

Johnson, 1992, p. 523

In Excerpt 2, the teacher recalled perceiving the student's continued errors as an indication of misunderstanding, and therefore continued to provide feedback, explain the concept, and check the student's knowledge. However, she also recalled her perceived ineffectiveness with these instructional actions, and commented on her mounting concern with not only the appropriateness of her teaching strategy, but also her inability to maintain control over the instructional activity.

Besides developing a useful heuristic through which to examine what teachers think about as they teach, it became obvious that these preservice ESL teachers interpreted their students' responses in uniquely different ways than would teachers in mainstream classrooms. For example, while mainstream elementary teachers perceived students' errors as a lack of students' attention or effort (Fogarty, Wang, & Creek, 1983), the ESL teachers in my study perceived students' errors as a lack of student understanding due to limited English language proficiency. In other words, what was seen as "fooling around" in one instructional context (L1) was seen as lack of understanding in another (L2). This suggested that it wasn't so much what students said or did that influenced teachers' interactive decisions, but how teachers interpreted what their students said and did that influenced their interactive decisions, and ultimately their classroom practice.

For me, one of the most important findings of this study was the realization that while teachers may think about similar things as they teach, how they think about these things, or teachers' interpretations of these instructional considerations, depends on and is shaped by who they are, what they know and believe, and the instructional contexts within which they work. It makes sense, then, that if we are to understand why teachers teach as they do, we must look at not only what they think about as they teach, we must also examine how they think about these things within the contexts of their own classrooms.

1 *EXPLORING YOUR OWN INSTRUCTIONAL CONSIDERATIONS*

Exploring your own instructional considerations will enable you to articulate why you teach the way you do; perhaps this realization will enable you to expand your knowledge of your own professional landscape and develop the robustness of your own reasoning.

In your reflective journal:

A. Reread the eight instructional considerations listed on page 57–58. Think about the most recent lesson you have taught and decide which combination of instructional considerations figured most prominently in your interactive decisions. Speculate on why you think this is so. What is it about yourself, your students, or the context within which you teach that influenced your interactive decisions?

B. Select an instructional consideration (listed on page 57–58) that you wish to explore in your own teaching. Audio-/videotape yourself teaching a lesson and then analyze the tape for the following:

- How do you deal with this instructional consideration?

- How do your students respond?

- How successful are you at dealing with the instructional consideration?

- What might be some alternative ways of dealing with this instructional consideration?

With other teachers:

C. Then discuss the analysis of your audio-/videotape with a classmate, a fellow teacher, or your instructor.

TEACHERS' INTERPRETATIONS

More recent research in the area of teacher cognition has convincingly argued that understanding teachers' interpretations is central to understanding teaching (Kagan, 1988; Shulman, 1986). This interpretivist view of teaching (Packer & Winne, 1995) argues that how teachers think about their teaching can only be understood as a joint function of both teachers and the places where teachers teach. Ulichny captures the interpretive qualities of teaching in her characterization of a teacher's methodology:

> [M]uch of a teacher's methodology resides in the way she interprets and acts on information from the ongoing classroom interactions. The interpretative framework she brings to the class is based on her past experiences as a teacher and learner, her professional knowledge and folk wisdom about teaching, and aspects of her personality. These factors shape the quality and kind of information she receives from the class. The ongoing interpretation of how well

the class is performing the task at hand influences immediate decisions on how to direct and redirect interaction as well as how to plan subsequent lessons and activities. (1996, p. 195)

In order for us to understand how teachers think about their teaching, we must explore teachers' reasoning where it occurs and our attention must be focused on how teachers conceptualize and respond to what occurs within those places. To do this we will explore teachers' interpretations as they emerge within the context of case-based methods and managing dilemmas.

CASE-BASED METHODS

Case-based methods (Shulman, 1992; Richert, 1987) have been widely used in mainstream teacher education as a means of revealing the complex variables that are considered as teachers sort out, make sense of, and justify the use of particular classroom practices. Cases are not general but instead specific to a particular context, so they are situated and include events within a particular time and place. Cases tend to be crafted in such as way as to provide examples of particular principles or theories, contain some sort of dramatic tension that must be resolved, and provide a rich description of the complexities of teachers' work. Case-based methods prepare teachers who can recognize what must be considered and done in any given classroom for themselves; in other words, initiating them into the complex processes of reasoning teaching.

Case-based methods have several other advantages. Unlike real classrooms, cases provide a safe environment for teachers to consider alternatives, granting them time and space to carefully consider all the issues embedded within an instructional situation. Case discussions are also social activities, in that teachers can get together in groups to discuss, reflect on, and analyze a case. Some have found that case-based discussions expand and deepen teachers' formal or content knowledge about what to teach (Barnett, 1991), as well as their practical knowledge about how to teach (Lundeberg & Scheurman, 1997). Others argue that teachers actively construct knowledge through case-based discussions using storied knowledge to anchor their more theoretical or abstract knowledge of teaching and learning (Carter, 1992, 1994; Sykes & Bird, 1992). Lundeberg & Scheurman argue that "repeated discussions of complex cases containing classroom dilemmas enabled preservice teachers to find new problems, rethink ideas, consider others' viewpoints and embed theoretical concepts from the perspective of the most recently completed area of study" (1997, p. 783). Shulman claims that cases are a powerful medium for teaching theory since "the value of the case for the learning of theory lies in the ways cases instantiate and contextualize principles through embedding them in vividly told stories" (1992, p. 5).

However, Spiro et al. warn that a single case used to illustrate a single theoretical or pedagogical principle can lead to misinterpretations when overgeneralized, and argue that multiple cases be used to treat the same principle "as a landscape that is explored by 'criss-crossing' it in many different directions" (1991, p. 178). Multiple cases permit teachers to explore a wider variety of settings and circumstances than can ever be experienced directly. This is not to say that case-based methods should replace field experiences. On the contrary,

Grossman argues that teachers need "a balance between the intensity of a few vivid experiences in the field and the vicarious explorations of a wide range of circumstances through cases" (1994, p. 15).

In spite of such limitations, case-based methods create opportunities for teachers to construct and use their knowledge about teaching in situated and interpretative ways and make explicit the complex nature of their reasoning. Moreover, reading, discussing, and even authoring cases create opportunities for teachers to talk about what they know within the contexts in which they work, foster reflection, and bring value to teachers' experiences and perspectives.

As part of a graduate-level seminar on the dynamics of communication in second language classrooms that I teach, students have the option of constructing a case about any aspect of their current or past teaching experiences. Below is one such case, written by a former student of mine, Sam, about a problem he faced in his own teaching. If you are familiar with my research, you have probably heard portions of this case before (see Johnson, 1996b; 1996c) since I have used this particular case in different contexts for different purposes. In fact, I use this case at least once a semester in my own master's in TESOL program. However, I include it here as illustrative of how this teacher conceptualizes, constructs an explanation for, and resolves a problem that he has identified in his own instructional context.

SAM'S CASE

THE CONTEXT:

Sam teaches ESL in an Adult Community Education Program in a mid-size university town. The program caters to two types of ESL students: newly settled immigrants who work for local manufacturing companies located on the outskirts of the town, and spouses of graduate students enrolled in degree programs at the university. The course is a beginning-level Conversational English class and meets twice a week in the evenings at a local community center. There are eleven students enrolled in this course. Five of the students, three males and two females, are Puerto Rican and are enrolled in the course as part of a work-based literacy program supported by their employer. Four of the students are Japanese women. Three are homemakers and one holds a clerical job in one of the undergraduate libraries on campus. The remaining two students are Russian and are husband and wife. They recently moved to the area through a church-based resettlement program. The husband works as a mechanic in a local gas station and the wife is a homemaker.

THE PROBLEM:

During the first two weeks of class, Sam noticed that the students with similar first languages tend to sit together and socialize with each other. During large group activities, the Spanish speakers tend to ask and answer most of the questions and dominate most of the student talk. Moreover, since the Spanish speakers work together they tend to talk about things that happen at work. The Japanese speakers tend to be very quiet. Sam feels strongly that everyone in his class should have equal opportunities to participate. It is through participation, Sam believes, that his students will acquire English and he realizes that for most of his students, this class is one of the few opportunities they have to actually speak English. Last week Sam tried an activity in which he paired up different first language speakers, but he found that the Spanish speakers dominated while the Japanese speakers sat quietly and when it was their turn to speak they appeared to be very uncomfortable. As soon as the activity was over, the students reorganized themselves according to first language groups again. While Sam is pleased with the Spanish speakers' eagerness to participate and does not want to squelch their opportunities to speak, he is very concerned about providing opportunities for the Japanese speakers to participate in class. Sam is also concerned about the Russian speakers because they tend to sit together and speak Russian to one another. Sam is at a loss for how to arrange his instructional activities to foster equal student participation.

Johnson, 1996b, pp. 12–13

CASE-BASED DISCUSSIONS

As a requirement of this project, Sam asked his classmates, who are also novice teachers, to consider the case and discuss possible solutions. The students began by talking about cultural differences in classroom participation. They suggested ways of making instructional activities predictable, since this helps minimize the risk that students may experience as they attempt to participate. They reminded Sam of the importance of students' feelings of competence, since the extent to which students are willing to participate depends on how they think their contributions will be received. They encouraged Sam to help his students make sense of new information by filtering it through what they already know—in other words, building on his students' prior knowledge. They encouraged Sam to explicitly tell his students exactly what is expected of them, perhaps even in the form of a concrete model or a demonstration. They reminded Sam of the importance of providing ample opportunity for students to prepare for an activity and to encourage students to use exploratory talk to formulate their ideas before having to make their ideas public in front of the class.

While discussing possible solutions for this case, Sam described three things that he planned to do with his students. First, in their dialogue journals, Sam explained his expectations for classroom participation and asked each student to describe his or her perceptions, feelings, and concerns about participating in class. Thus, he initiated and sustained a private dialogue with each student about classroom participation. Second, he devoted some class time to an open discussion about classroom participation. He explained why he feels it is important for all students to participate in class and he allowed the students to describe their perceptions of classroom participation. As a result of this discussion, the class generated a set of participation rules that everyone agreed to follow for the remainder of the semester. These had to do with rules for turn-taking in both small and large group discussions. Third, he attempted to make his instructional activities predictable so as to foster more student participation. Below is a portion of Sam's solution, written in the context of one particular lesson, that illustrates how he organized his instruction to foster more equal student participation.

THE SOLUTION:

While planning a lesson on polite ways of making and accepting invitations, Sam recalled that his students are much more willing to participate when they are given an opportunity to relate what they are learning to their own experiences. Therefore, he planned to begin the lesson with a large group discussion in which he would ask his students to share their own personal experiences of having to make and/or accept invitations. However, since his previous attempts at large group discussions were not very successful, (i.e., the Puerto Rican students tend to dominate while the others sit quietly) Sam decided to ask the students to complete a journal assignment (prior to class) in which they were to write about their own personal experiences either making and/or accepting invitations. He hoped the Japanese and Russian students would be more willing to participate in the large group discussion if they had an opportunity to rehearse what they would be expected to say in writing. Sam also wanted his students to know exactly what was expected of them, so before assigning the journal assignment, he shared his own personal example of when he reluctantly accepted an invitation for a blind date. His model contained some background information about the social situation and the status of the speakers, and illustrated how he accepted the invitation.

On the day of the lesson, Sam placed his students in pairs and asked them to share their journal assignments with one another. He hoped this activity would give them an opportunity to rehearse telling their personal experiences before being asked to speak in front of the entire class. He also encouraged the students to ask questions or request further information from their partners if some aspect of the story was unclear. He then explained that when they were finished they would be expected to retell their partner's story to the class. Sam decided to use a retelling activity because he felt it would reinforce listening comprehension skills and generate more authentic language.

After the retelling activity, Sam played three audio-taped dialogues that illustrate making and accepting invitations in different social contexts. Knowing that his students' listening comprehension skills were weak, Sam broke the listening task into smaller parts, assigning individual students the task of listening for one specific piece of information. For example, two students were asked to listen for how the speaker introduced the invitation, two other students were asked to listen for how the actual invitation was made, and two others were to listen for how the listener accepted the invitation. After each dialogue, Sam allowed the two students to compare what they had heard, and then to share that information with the class.

As a final activity, Sam placed the students in pairs and asked them to create a scenario in which they had to make and accept an invitation. Since, once again, Sam felt it was important for his students to see a model of what they were expected to do, Sam and a student volunteer modeled a scenario for the class. In preparation for the performance activity, Sam placed two pairs together in a group of four, and ask each pair to perform their scenario for the other. He then asked the pairs to switch and, once again, perform their scenario for a new pair. Once the pairs had rehearsed their scenarios several times, he asked for volunteers to perform their scenario in front of the entire class. During the performance activity, Sam asked the class to listen for how the speaker introduced the invitation, how the actual invitation was made, and how the listener accepted the invitation. This information became the basis for the follow-up discussion after each pair performed their scenario.

Johnson, 1996b, p. 13

Embedded in Sam's case we see what he thinks about and how he thinks about his teaching within his own instructional context. To resolve this problem, Sam had to articulate the exact nature of the problem and why he saw it as a problem. He had to formulate a solution that was appropriate for this particular group of students within this particular context. Sam had to reflect on his own knowledge and beliefs about teachers, students, teaching, and learning. He had to critically analyze his own teaching. He had to consider and implement a range of instructional strategies that would be sensitive not only to the unique needs and learning styles of his students, but also to the social factors that affect their learning. By writing this case, Sam had to articulate his reasoning, and by reading and responding to this case(see below), we are able to understand how Sam's reasoning shaped his classroom practices.

2 CASE-BASED DISCUSSIONS

Engaging in case-based discussions will help you reveal the complex nature of teachers' reasoning. Such discussions can generate insights into the complex variables that teachers consider as they sort out, make sense of, and justify the use of particular classroom practices. In addition, case-based discussions can help you see alternative instructional strategies for dealing with complex problems that occur in classrooms.

In your reflective journal:

A.   Reread Sam's case. Reflect on how you would have resolved this problem. Make a list of alternative instructional strategies for resolving such a problem.

With other teachers:

B. Exchange and discuss your lists of alternative strategies for resolving this problem. What sort of similarities and differences are there among your lists? Why do you think this is so? How realistic are your solutions? What obstacles might emerge as you try to institute your solutions?

C. Reflect on what you learned from responding to and discussing Sam's case. Describe how you will apply what you have learned from this case to your own teaching.

MANAGING DILEMMAS

Many of the teachers with whom I work become discouraged by problems they face in their classrooms that never really seem to go away. They complain that these problems not only inhibit their teaching but also limit students' opportunities for language learning. Lampert offers an alternative way of conceptualizing the sorts of problems that my teachers complain about. It is a conception of teachers as managers of dilemmas rather than problem solvers.

> The image of the teacher as dilemma manager accepts conflict as a continuing condition with which persons can learn to cope. [I]n addition to defending against and choosing among conflicting expectations, . . . the dilemma manager accepts conflict as endemic and even useful to her work rather than seeing it as a burden that needs to be eliminated. (1985, p. 192)

Exploring teachers' reasoning through the rubric of dilemma manager enables us to understand teachers' classroom practices as being guided by the notion of "it depends." If we characterize teaching as managing dilemmas, then how teachers understand a particular dilemma, the way in which they choose to manage that dilemma, and the consequences of managing it in one particular way over another give us tremendous insight into the complexity of teachers' reasoning.

Native Language Use in the ESL Classroom

Several years ago, a novice teacher described during a weekly practicum meeting that no matter what she did, a group of freshman female Puerto Rican students continued to speak Spanish to one another during her ESL composition class. She had first asked them politely to speak English in class, and later even threatened them with grade reductions. She had split them up around the room and grouped them with speakers of other languages. But despite all her efforts, she complained that they continued to speak Spanish to one another during class.

This incident intrigued me, not because her students were using their native language in an English language class, but because this novice teacher saw it as a problem that needed to be solved. For our next meeting, I asked this group of six novice teachers to read the article by Lampert from which the quotation above was taken in which she characterizes teachers as managers of dilemmas that can never really be solved, but instead are simply managed. At our next meeting, we decided to talk about native language use in the classroom and to conceptualize it through Lampert's notion of a dilemma that might be managed rather than a problem that needed to be solved.

The first step in our analysis was to explore why native language use in the class was considered a problem in the first place. Prompted by a sincere yet pointed question asked by one of her fellow novice teachers, "Why do you care if they use Spanish?" we embarked on a lengthy conversation about our beliefs about second language learning and teaching and our memories of our own second language learning experiences. Interestingly, this teacher was actually a native speaker of Spanish and had studied English in classrooms in which the use of Spanish was strictly forbidden. This rule was so rigidly enforced that students were fined each time they spoke Spanish in class. This teacher felt this sort of classroom-based immersion forced her to learn English, believing that if she had been allowed to use Spanish, it would have hindered her progress in English.

As our weekly conversations continued, we discovered that this teacher was also concerned about the other students in her class, who she thought might feel left out by the Spanish speakers. From here we began to focus on ways this teacher might manage students' native language use in the classroom. One teacher suggested that every time the students used Spanish, one member of the group should be required to translate it into English for the entire class. Another teacher suggested creating some activities in which students would be encouraged to use their native languages in small groups and then present their ideas in English. Someone suggested that this teacher take note of what these students said in Spanish since they might be using Spanish to help one another learn English.

On another occasion, we had a lengthy discussion about the social function that Spanish seemed to play for this group of students. This is, within our largely rural, middle-class, white university population, where Spanish speakers were clearly minorities and where no local Spanish-speaking community exists, the use of Spanish among these students seemed to solidify their social identification with one another and against the majority university community. In addition, we talked about the linguistic and situational context within which this teacher's classroom existed—namely, the difference between our ESL learning environment (where students were exposed to English outside the classroom) and an EFL environment (where exposure to English is generally limited to classroom interactions).

Our conversation about native language use continued over the course of the fifteen-week practicum. Each time the issue came up we attempted to analyze the consequences of managing this dilemma in one way or another. For example, if this teacher ignored native language use by her Puerto Rican students, she worried that her Asian students would feel left out. If she required a translation for every Spanish utterance, this took time away from her instructional activities. If she encouraged students to use their native language for a specific instructional activity, she felt guilty that they were not using English in what was supposed to be an English class.

Near the end of the semester it was becoming apparent to this teacher and to the other teachers in the group that a few Spanish exchanges between friends in class did not constitute a major stumbling block to learning English in this particular setting. It also became evident that how this teacher had conceptualized this dilemma and how she chose to manage it would have different consequences for different students. However, eventually the entire group and, in particular, this teacher seemed to come to terms with this dilemma. In one of her final journal entries she wrote:

> After all I've been through with this group (the Puerto Rican students), I've really begun to like them and I think they like me. I must admit that I still find it distracting when they use Spanish in class but I understand why they do this now and I finally realized that it has nothing to do with me. This is who they are, and who am I to change that. The problem didn't go away but it really isn't a problem anymore and it was me who had to come to terms with that.

What was once conceptualized as a problem to be solved had now been recast as a dilemma that could be managed. As Lampert would suggest, this novice teacher needed to recognize that such problems are endemic and even useful if understood and responded to within the complex landscape in which teachers work. For this novice teacher, the completeness of her understanding of herself, her students, and the context within which she was teaching shaped how she understood and eventually learned to manage this dilemma. For her, conceptualizing her own teaching as managing dilemmas reinforced the notion that knowing what to do in any classroom depends on a host of considerations, and the ways in which she came to recognize, interpret, and respond to these considerations rests at the core of both learning to teach and understanding her own teaching.

---

3 REFLECTING ON DILEMMAS

Investigations

Most teachers face dilemmas in the classroom that seem difficult, if not impossible, to solve. The first step in managing any dilemma is to identify the context within which it occurs, articulate the exact nature of the problem, and recognize a range of acceptable solutions. The following Investigations will help you do this.

In your reflective journal:

A. Reflect on a "dilemma" that you face in your teaching (for example, the use of L1 in an ESL class). Write a one-page description of the dilemma, including how you are currently dealing with this dilemma. If possible, share your description with a colleague. Then generate a list of alternative ways that you might manage this dilemma. Analyze each point on your list and try to determine the consequences of managing the dilemma in this particular way.

---

4 RESPONDING TO CASES

Responding to cases creates opportunities for you to examine problems that arise in classrooms and to explore the reasoning that shapes how you and other teachers conceptualize, construct explanations for, and resolve such problems. Embedded in the experience of responding to cases is the opportunity to make explicit the reasoning that shapes teachers' practices.

A. Each of the four cases below contains the following:

- The context: A brief description of the context, giving background information about the setting, the students, and the class

- The problem: A description of the problem from the teacher's perspective and his or her perception of how this instructional consideration is central to the problem

B. Select and read one of the four cases. Discuss what you understand to be the central problem embedded in the case. Make a list of alternative instructional strategies for resolving this problem and describe how you would resolve it. Discuss what you learned from responding to this case. Describe how you will you apply what you have learned from this case to your own teaching.

CASE 1

Grade Level: *Elementary*

Dilemma(s): *Multiskill/Proficiency Levels*
Student Affective Needs

THE CONTEXT:

Miss Allison teaches ESL in an elementary school in a small southern town neighboring a small university. The school district has very few ESL students and the school has not yet figured out how to best meet their needs. Currently, all ESL students are "immersed" in regular classrooms with their peers. However, because many teachers have complained that the ESL students lag behind the other children in reading and writing skills, the former are pulled out of their classrooms three times a week for two hours to work on literacy skills with Miss Allison. The students include two Russian boys, one in third grade and one in fourth; one Japanese girl in fourth grade; one German girl in second grade; and one Korean boy in third grade.

THE PROBLEM:

Miss Allison has found it very difficult to choose appropriate reading and writing tasks for this group of children due to their different native languages and widely varying reading and writing skill levels. The German girl reads English very well for her age, but she is still behind the two fourth-graders and has extreme difficulty with writing assignments. The Korean boy has excellent reading and writing skills in his first language, but has had much less exposure to English than the other children in the group and is struggling to keep up with the content of the lessons in his regular classroom. The two Russian boys seem to read at grade level in English; however, they are very resistant to writing or speaking English and avoid doing so when they are in their regular classrooms. The Japanese girl is functioning almost completely satisfactorily in her regular classroom, but participates in the ESL classes due to her parents' concern that she will fall behind her English-speaking peers academically if she does not learn to sound more native when she writes and speaks.

While struggling to accommodate these differing skill levels, Miss Allison is also very concerned about her students' social well-being. Because the town has no international families, the other students in the school are not used to having class-mates who are not "American" in their classrooms. The town harbors many south-ern conservative attitudes and the children hear a lot of racist and anti-immigration propaganda outside of school. With the exception of the German girl, whose accent is fairly undetectable, the ESL students are made fun of by their classmates, who call them names and say that they "don't know how to talk right."

The Russian boys pose a particular problem because while they are normally very talkative at home or with one another, they have learned to remain quiet in their regular classrooms to avoid being mocked by the other children. When they come to Miss Allison's class, they are so happy to have each other to speak to that they often talk loudly to each other in Russian, distracting the other stu-dents and themselves from the tasks Miss Allison attempts to carry out.

Miss Allison's goal for these children is to improve their overall literacy skills, but also to help them feel at home in their new school and feel good about them-selves in general.

Case 2

Grade Level: *Secondary*

Dilemma(s): *Content-Based Instruction*
Student Motivation & Involvement

The Context:
Mr. Mills has been a high school biology teacher in a suburb of a major north-eastern city for ten years. Recently there has been some concern about the fact that the ESL students in the district consistently perform poorly on standardized science tests. This year Mr. Mills has been asked to teach a separate biology class for the ESL students in order to focus on their special needs. Administrators hope that if these students are given specialized instruction they will learn the scientific content more adequately and achieve higher scores on the district's standardized tests. Mr. Mills's class has twenty students. Ten of them are of Hispanic origin, eight are from China, one is Korean, and one is Russian.

The Problem:
Mr. Mills feels that he is struggling to satisfy competing interests in a limited amount of time. He is aware of the topics that will be tested on the standardized biology test at the end of the year. Mr. Mills feels that in order for these students to perform well on the test, they need to learn a tremendous amount of special-ized biology vocabulary and concepts. His students are not interested in this material or motivated to learn it, especially because the majority of them do not

aspire to attend college—it is doubtful that some will even finish high school. Whenever Mr. Mills attempts to address this sort of information the students become bored and sometimes get disruptive. He feels that to continue would be a waste of time because he believes they will never learn material that they are not interested in.

However, Mr. Mills has noticed that the students are not completely uninterested in the topic of biology. On a couple of occasions, his students became very involved when he conducted some simple experiments that demonstrated various biological processes that affect the functioning of the human body. They also seemed interested when Mr. Mills introduced the topics of genetics, evolution, and biological engineering.

Unfortunately, the subject matter that seems to be most interesting to the students does not coincide with the material that will be examined on the standardized test. Mr. Mills feels he is in the position of having to decide whether to focus on helping the students become familiar with the topics that will be tested or to address the subject matter that they seem to be genuinely curious about.

Case 3

Grade Level: *University*

Dilemma(s): *Student Participation*
Appropriateness of Teaching Strategy

THE CONTEXT:

Sue teaches an academic writing course for ESL students who are about to begin a four-year undergraduate degree program at a large university. The course is intended to prepare students for the academic writing tasks they will face in the university by familiarizing them with the rhetorical structures and academic writing skills necessary to complete academic essays and research papers. Sue is also expected to address her students' grammatical difficulties and provide instruction that will help their writing sound more native. The class meets twice a week for seventy-five minutes. There are twenty-five students enrolled in the course. Two students are from Puerto Rico, one male and one female, and one male student is from Colombia. The rest of the students are from Asian backgrounds (Chinese, Korean, Japanese); about half are female and half are male. While all of Sue's students have serious language-related problems evident in their writing, many of them actually graduated from American high schools.

THE PROBLEM:

While teaching this course in the past, Sue has been successful at engaging her students in group discussions about their reading and writing assignments. Her "discussion" style of teaching has enabled her students not only to learn about academic reading and writing but to improve their oral communication skills as well. However, with this particular group of students Sue has experienced difficulty initiating fruitful class discussions. The two Puerto Rican students speak with ease and sound much like native speakers; they tend to dominate any type of open class discussion. Many of the Asian students in the class have culture-related discomfort with free classroom discussions and are greatly intimidated by the high level of English-speaking proficiency displayed by the two Puerto Rican students.

Although Sue has asked her two Puerto Rican students to remain quiet at times in order for the other students to have a chance to participate, they continue to dominate most class discussions. It seems that they have great difficulty refraining from commenting, especially when everyone else in the class is very quiet. When Sue asked the Asian students why they didn't participate more in class, she heard two main reasons: (1) they are embarrassed because they can't speak English very well, and (2) they don't like to speak in class and don't understand why they should be required to speak in a writing course.

While Sue does not want to abandon her teaching style of learning through discussions, she has found the classroom dynamics with this group so difficult that she is considering structuring the classroom activities around individual writing tasks instead.

CASE 4

Grade Level: *Adult*

Dilemma(s): *Low-level Proficiency*
Student Motivation and Involvement

THE CONTEXT:

Karla teaches ESL to Spanish-speaking adults in a major city in southern Florida. The class is free for students thanks to donations made by various church and community associations in the city. Long-time church groups organized the fundraising to support the English classes because of their concern about increasing social problems in the area related to the large influx of poor immigrants from Central America. Community and church leaders hoped that English classes would encourage the newly settled Spanish speakers to become contributing members of the community by helping them acquire the English language skills necessary to find employment. The English classes have been well advertised and focus on English for both the workplace and life skills. The classes meet three nights a week in a local community center; however, attendance has been inconsistent, with a different group of adults each night.

THE PROBLEM:

Karla has found it difficult to deal with the informality and irregularity of this teaching situation. Because of the unpredictable attendance of the students she does not know how best to plan her lessons. She does not want the classes to be too repetitive for the few who do attend regularly but she also wants to be sure that all those who attend have their most pressing needs met. Karla has tried to encourage her students to come to class more consistently. Often they say they will, but then after a few sessions they stop attending again. It seems that their motivation to learn English wanes, first because there are enough other Spanish speakers in the area to meet their communication needs, and second because they have already begun to experience negative feelings from the English-speaking community in the city.

An additional problem is that many students can only attend the English classes if they bring their small children. Child care services are either not available or too expensive for most of them. The children are sometimes loud and disruptive and distract their parents from the activities of the class.

Moreover, Karla has difficulty understanding what her students' questions and problems are. While her students tend to perform classroom tasks with reasonable success, they later complain that they were unable to transfer these skills outside the classroom setting. Because most of her students know very little English and Karla knows only very basic Spanish, they have trouble communicating with each other about complicated topics or their personal concerns.

---

5 *CREATING A CASE*

Creating a case allows you to explore problems that arise in your own classroom and to articulate the reasoning that shapes how you conceptualize, construct explanations for, and resolve such problems.

A. Create a case in which you examine a dilemma that you faced in a past or current teaching context. Your case should include the following:

Context: Briefly describe the context, giving background information about the setting, the students, and the class. In addition, describe the specific instructional consideration that you have selected to be the focus of this case.

Dilemma: Describe the dilemma as clearly as possible. Try to provide both the teacher's and the students' perspectives on the dilemma. Note the instructional considerations that are central to the dilemma.

Solution: Describe how you managed or resolved this dilemma. Note your instructional considerations and to what extent you changed your teaching practices to deal with this dilemma.

Responses: Give your case to a classmate, a fellow teacher, or your instructor and discuss the context, the dilemma, and your proposed solution. Then, ask him or her to comment on how he or she would have managed this dilemma. Discuss alternative ways of dealing with this dilemma.

B. Share your case with other teachers. Ask them to respond to your management of this dilemma. Encourage them to offer alternative instructional strategies for managing this dilemma.

Suggested Readings

There are many good books on the use of case-based methods in teacher education. Judith Shulman's book *Case methods in teacher education* (New York: Teachers College Press, 1992) is an edited collection of articles written about the use and misuse of case-based methods. For a collection of actual cases that can certainly be adapted to second language teaching contexts, I recommend Gordon Greenwood and Forrest Parkay's book *Case studies for teacher decision making* (New York: Random House, 1989). For an example of case-based methods in second language teacher education, I recommend B. Conley's description of "Using Case Studies in Teacher Education" in *TESOL new ways in teacher education*, Alexandria, VA: 1993, 29–35.

Teacher reflection and reflective teaching continue to be popular "buzz" words in our profession, but for the classics on how practitioners use their knowledge in action, I recommend Donald Schon's books *The reflective practitioner: How professionals think in action* (New York: Basic Books, 1983) and *Educating the reflective practitioner* (San Francisco, CA: Joosey-Bass, 1987). In the early 1980's, Schon's books articulated a view of teacher reflection that dramatically changed traditional teacher education practices in North America. And finally, Margaret Lampert's 1985 article "How Do Teachers Manage to Teach? Perspectives on Problems in Practice" (*Harvard Educational Review* 55 (2): 178–194) is an excellent example of how reflection on classroom practice helps us understand the complex ways in which teachers manage the dilemmas the face in their daily activities.

A PROLOGUE TO THREE CASES OF REASONING IN ACTION

In the next three chapters we enter the lives, minds, and classrooms of three very different teachers teaching very different students in very different instructional contexts. Each welcomes us into his or her classroom and makes explicit for us the complex ways in which he or she conceptualizes, constructs explanations for, and responds to what occurs within that professional landscape. In reading these three cases, our goal is to understand the reasoning that undergirds these teachers' practices. Through narratives that represent their knowledge and beliefs, transcripts of their actual teaching practices, and reflective comments on those practices, we see that teachers' reasoning occurs within a rich social context, supported by what teachers know about their students, influenced by teachers' own knowledge and beliefs about what is important for their students to learn, and shaped, in large part, by knowing their own instructional contexts. Bound up in teachers' reasoning is the accumulation of their experiences, knowledge, and beliefs about learning and teaching through which they make sense of the actions and interactions that take place around them as they teach. Everything teachers consider, every decision they make, and every interaction they participate in depends on the ways in which they interpret, construct explanations for, and respond to the actions and interactions that occur with their students, in their classrooms, and in their schools.

6

REASONING TEACHING IN AN ELEMENTARY ESL PROGRAM

KEN: TEACHING STUDENTS TO THINK

When you first walk into Ken's elementary-level ESL classroom you get the odd sensation of being in a warm space with cold surroundings. In part this is due to the twenty-foot ceiling and the drab olive curtains that hang to the floor, carving out classroom space for the school's two ESL teachers. Then there are the cement walls and movable partitions covered with brightly colored posters of insects, trees, and animals, students' work hung proudly on every available inch of space, and modular tables placed in a semicircle facing a tiny blackboard at what one assumes is the front of the room. Unless you were in Ken's room early in the morning, after lunch, or late in the afternoon, you wouldn't know that behind the curtains are the school's garbage storage bins, mounds of cleaning materials, and the janitors' lockers. Until recently this space was the janitor's closet, but when an influx of Cambodian, Vietnamese, and Hispanic students entered the district, it was partitioned into makeshift ESL classrooms.

Ken's classes are considered "pull-out" since all ESL students in the school are mainstreamed in regular elementary classes, spending only a portion of the day—depending on their level of English language proficiency—in Ken's class. All of Ken's classes are content-based—that is, students learn English through learning about science, social studies, or language arts. Moreover, the content of Ken's instruction matches but is not identical to that of the regular classroom teachers. So while a regular classroom teacher may be covering a science unit on insects, Ken's pull-out ESL science lessons will also focus on the general topic of insects. However, instead of using the regular classroom textbook or commercial ESL materials, Ken finds supplemental reading materials that focus on the same topic and he constructs different sorts of language and learning activities that emphasize basic literacy skills.

Ken came to his current teaching position eight years ago with a wealth of knowledge about and experiences with language learning and teaching. He modestly admits to his facility for learning other languages, crediting his ability to mimic other people's accents and his own interest in other cultures with enabling him to learn and speak three languages besides English. He has taught EFL in Iran, Japan, Spain, and Mexico and ESL in the United States, mostly to adults, yet he credits his own experiences as a father with learning how to teach children. He describes his conception of himself as a teacher:

I try to meet kids where their needs are . . . at the point that they're at, and help them move forward from wherever that is. And I think I bring a certain amount of knowledge of my field, knowledge of the students and knowledge of language. I think I bring creativity in how I deal with issues to that point of where kids are at. And I think I bring flexibility in that whatever we need to do we do. But it's all focused on the point of where kids are at. And seeing where they need to go and helping them move forward.

Ken's conception of himself as a teacher is firmly grounded in his experiences as a language learner. He recalls responding to language teachers who challenged him, who actively engaged him in the language learning process, who expected him to look and act and talk as if he knew the language, who held high expectations for him yet cared about him as a unique individual. While getting his master's degree in TESOL, Ken recalled he was forced to reflect on

what we believed to be true about language, what we believed to be true about learning, and what we believed to be true about teaching. And then trying to take that with us on the internship and actually teach and reflect on, "Well this is what you said you believed in the course, is what you're doing now a reflection of what you said you believed?" And often I found that what I thought I believed is not what I did, and then I had to decide, was I kidding myself about my beliefs, or do I just have to learn how to express my beliefs through what I did. And often I found that they were poorly thought through . . . they were theoretical, as opposed to personal beliefs. And I ended up changing a little bit of both to get where I wanted to be.

Ken describes the most difficult aspect of being a second language teacher in this particular instructional context as the language weaknesses that his students bring with them to school. He describes their life experiences as limited, their first language literacy skills as extremely weak, and their home situations as frequently tumultuous. He describes his students' difficulties as his difficulties, adding that the rewards of teaching are when some or any of these difficulties are overcome as his students are successful using and learning the English language. Yet, if you spend some time in Ken's classroom, you will quickly realize that he is not just interested in having his students learn English. An underlying goal that permeates Ken's every instructional decision and action is to enable these students to think critically and independently about what they experience, read, and write. Ken explains:

It's really important that kids be able to think independently at a given task. I keep asking kids how and where they got the answer, just to help them slowly construct a schema of knowing. When I read something like this, I know I need to look at the picture, and I need to go to the words. If the teacher isn't able to get around to them a lot, they need to be able to figure that out on their own from this point on or in the future. And so, I keep trying to have kids reflect on how they got the answer, where they got the answer, why did they pick that particular answer. So that if they do it enough in response to my questions, they might get an image of me asking them, "Why did you get that answer?" And without me around, or another teacher asking them that same question, to help them to build that schema of how to look for information.

KEN: WHY DO BUGS HAVE COLOR?

On this particular morning, the lesson topic is insect coloration; specifically, why bugs have color. Moments after the bell rings, fourth- and fifth-grade students begin to rush into Ken's room. One young boy proudly hands Ken a clear plastic salad container filled with green grass, rocks, and dirt. He excitedly describes how he found some bugs in his backyard and brought them in to show the rest of the class. Seizing this opportunity, Ken quiets the class by holding up the container, studying it carefully as he searches for the bugs. As he squints at the bottom of the container, he repeats a student's question, "Is this bug an insect or not?" Eager hands go up. Someone calls out "Yes"; another student shouts "No!" Ken calmly talks the class through a series of questions that review the characteristics of an insect.

CLASSROOM EPISODE #1

K: Is that it right there? I think you can just see the bottom of this under there now. A little bit later there's going to be time for kids to get up. If you look under there, you can probably see it. Phan asked if that's an insect or not. What are the questions that we could ask ourselves about is it an insect? What does it have to have?

S1: Three body parts.

K: Three body parts and what's it going to have?

S2: I know, I know—six legs.

K: Six legs. What's it going to have?

S3: Antenna.

K: Antenna, and it might have what on the back?

Ss: Wings.

K: Wings—how many pairs usually?

Ss: Two.

K: Two—so, if it has the six legs, with the three body parts, and an antenna, we'll know it's an insect. If it doesn't, then we'll know it's not an insect, and we have to figure out then what it is, if it's not an insect.

Ken's underlying goal of enabling his students to think critically and independently about what they are learning is often modeled through the way he talks. Ken describes this as "thinking without being so explicit"; in other words, he talks his students through a series of probing questions that force them to think through their ideas and critically evaluate their answers. Ken's questions model a way of thinking about new information, a way of thinking that he knows will be expected of these students in their regular elementary classrooms. Holding up the salad container for all to see, Ken continues.

CLASSROOM EPISODE #2

K: So, what I'm going to do, is I'm going to bring in some ice tomorrow, or Wednesday, whichever one. . . . I'll get some crushed ice. We'll put this in the ice for a while. What do you think is going to happen if we take this and put it in some ice? What do you think will happen if we put ice in there?

S1: They will fall asleep.

K: Kind of fall asleep. Their body will get s-l-o-w-e-r and s-l-o-w-e-r, and they'll stop moving. And then we can pick it up, we can look at it, we can look at it real close. Could you look at it real close when it's moving all around? It will be um, um all over the place. But when it's been in the ice and it's gotten really cold, then its body will stop moving, and you can look at it. Then when it warms up— what's going to happen? Did we kill it? How many think if we put it in ice we're going to kill it? Anybody think we're going to kill it? You might think that. Who thinks we're not going to kill it? You're all right. We don't kill it. You know what happens. We're going to put it back in there, and as it warms up, it's not even going to know what happened. It's going to start to scoot around again. That's the way you can study insects.

Ken's reflective comments (student motivation and involvement):

[A]It's important for kids to work on thinking. [B]One of the things that they need to do is learn how to ask themselves questions about things that are mentioned, and to reflect on why might somebody do that. [C]And rather than just say, "I'm going to get ice, and I'm going to put the insects in it because it makes the insects stop moving," [D]it gives the kids a chance to see if they can draw on their own experience of being cold and slowing down, or thinking about it to try to use their own experience to guess, [E]rather than just be waiting to be told. [F]This gets them into it, gets them thinking, gets them reflecting on what they know about this. It forces them to get involved in thinking about the ideas.

Ken explains (D and F) that asking students to draw on their own experiences directly involves them in thinking about this idea in a more personal and, he hopes, a more meaningful way. Embedded in Ken's reasoning (A and B) is his underlying belief in the importance of developing critical thinking skills in these students. Hence his decision to ask his students to predict what might happen if he put this bug on ice was made with consideration for student motivation and involvement and remains consistent with his beliefs about the importance of critical thinking skills in language learning and teaching. Moreover, Ken positions himself and his teaching against the traditional image of teachers as givers of knowledge. He takes on the voice of such teachers (C), those who see themselves as providers of information as opposed to facilitators of students' ways of relating to and learning about new information. In a sense he is framing himself and his teaching as different from other teachers—teachers he may have had as a student, other teachers in his school, or simply Ken's conception of teachers in general.

Placing the salad container aside, Ken directs the students' attention to a crude colored paper cut-out of a red flower with a red insect crawling up it next to a brightly colored yellow-and-black spotted beetle crawling up a green leaf. He asks the class to look carefully for two insects. A student in the front seat leaps out of his seat, eager to point out the barely noticeable red insect crawling up the red flower.

CLASSROOM EPISODE #3

K: Now, I made believe this weekend that I was Mother Nature, and I made two insects. Can you see? This is one insect, right? Where's the other one? You can see this one pretty easy. Where's the other one? Does anyone see the other one? It's awful hard to see, Tuin, do you see? Just tell me where it is.

S1: On that red thing.

K: There's two red things—which one?

S1: That one.

K: Which one is that one?

S1: On the right.

K: On the right, the one on the right. And where is it. Do you see it? There it is.

Ken's reflective comments (student language skill and ability):

[A]One of the things that a lot of these kids can't do very well is use language to describe, to give meaning to everything that they see. They still rely on a lot of gesturing and again [B]English is his [Tuin's] stronger language; he speaks English better than Khmer, so he doesn't have the wherewithal to say, "The one on, it's on the one on the right," or "It's on that side." He has to physically get up and point to it. [C]So you know it's important to take those times to let the kids, [D]rather than make it a special lesson, to have a child be able to practice how to describe things with normal everyday language. It's really important for these kids.

Obviously Ken knows his students well. He not only knows their individual language skills and abilities, but at times he seems to take on their voices (B); talking as they might talk, thinking as they might think. It's almost as if he tries to see the world as they do. Given what Ken knows about his students' language skills and abilities in general (A) and those of this student in particular (B), he insists that the student use language to locate the hidden insect. He explains this decision by contrasting his actions with what might be thought of as traditional language teaching (D), in which language is taught as isolated units or based on grammatical structures, and reiterates (C) what he believes is important for language learning and teaching.

Ken reviews the concept of camouflage from yesterday's lesson by contrasting it with the second reason why insects have color: advertising. In the midst of Ken's explanation, one student calls out that he thinks the yellow-and-black spotted insect on the green leaf is a stinkbug. Ken seizes this opportunity to use a student's contribution to illustrate the concept of advertising.

CLASSROOM EPISODE #4

K: Now, an insect that is colored like that because of the flower that it's on—what would that be called? What's the reason that insect is that color? Phan?

S1: Camouflage.

K: Camouflage, that's the first one. (Writes on the board.) And the camouflage, as you know, is coloring for protection. If you were a bird flying around, would you be able to see that easily?

Ss: No

K: But what about that one? Now, was I, Mother Nature, making a big mistake making a bug that color? Is that hard to see?

Ss: No.

K: So why do you think this bug is this bright color walking around on a green piece of grass? What do you think? If you were a bird flying around, which one would you see really fast? He's so bright; he's so easy to see. Phan?

S1: I think, maybe, this kind of bug is a little bit like a stinkbug.

K: And why would a stinkbug be so brightly colored? Everyone know what a stinkbug is? What does it sound like it does? Stinkbug?

S2: Stinks.

K: It stinks. Yeah, if you go over and you bother it, you go "oooh," and you go away quickly because it stinks, because nobody likes to bother a stink bug, stink bugs don't have to hide.

Ken's reflective comments (student motivation and involvement):

[A]The answer that boy gave about the stink bug, or why this particular bug was brightly colored, was an example of what the answer was supposed to be. [B]So I had to bridge the—you know—validating the intent of the answer with bridging that into the actual answer. [C]And, so, it's important to validate the child being willing to stick his hand up in front of the class and say, "Oh I know the answer to that." [D]And, in a sense, he did, but he might not have had the language to explain it clearly, or he might not even know the difference between an example and a reason. And, so, [E]trying to keep the discussion flowing and keep everybody willing to raise their hand, if they want, but [F]making sure that the right information gets explained.

Keeping students motivated and involved in the lesson (C and E) is clearly important to Ken. Yet he knows his students so well (D) that even though this student did not answer Ken's question (A), he did offer an acceptable alternative—an example—that Ken recognizes and validates (C) as a way to encourage involvement in the lesson. However, Ken remains mindful that the appropriate subject matter content gets covered (F), and therefore sees his role as one of creating a bridge between what his students know and what he is trying to teach them (C). Thus, Ken must balance the need to keep students willing to participate while at the same time ensuring that the content of the lesson is covered.

As he continues with his explanation of advertising Ken maintains a fast pace, scanning the faces of each student, motioning to the hands that seem to be continually raised, letting others shout out answers, and calling on those who seem to be drifting. Most of the students seem intrigued. A few can hardly stay in their seats. But one quiet girl is resting her head on her hands and seems lost in her own thoughts.

CLASSROOM EPISODE #5

K: Sometimes when bugs have bright colors, that means that they are poison. This is a poison bug, and, if I'm a bird and I'm flying around and I see that bug, what do I think?

S1: You shouldn't go eat it.

K: Shouldn't go eat it because it's poison.

S2: It's a warning.

K: Okay, I'm going to name it something else. It is a warning, but I'm going to call it "advertising." This might be my own word, by the way, but I want you to understand very well. Do you know what advertising is?

S3: Yeah.

K: On TV—what's your favorite show. Ivana, what do you like to watch on TV?

S4: I like cartoons.

K: Cartoons—and when you're watching the cartoons, do they stop sometimes . . . the cartoon—the cartoon is over and they try to sell you some toy or something, or some food?

S5: Yeah.

K: Yeah. That's advertising.

Ken's reflective comments (instructional management):

> [A]That girl was not paying attention, and I wanted her to be a part of the discussion. [B]So I asked her, with her name in the flow of the question, [C]something that was going to lead me back into what I was taking about. So she got the clue, [D]"I have to pay attention," and [E]I was able to use whatever her answer was to talk about what I was really trying to get at.

Even when Ken considers instructional management issues, as in this episode where a student is not paying attention (A), he does so by encouraging the student to become involved in the lesson. Instead of explicitly admonishing this student, Ken simply uses the student's name in the flow of his question (B) and then takes up what the student has to offer and goes on to relate it to the subject content of the lesson.

It is obvious that Ken expects his students to be actively involved in class discussions. There seems to be a comfortable balance between students calling out answers and others being called on. Yet participation is not forced. When a student fails to respond to one of Ken's questions, he calmly waits for what seems to an outsider to be an inordinate amount of time, and then offers the student the option of passing on his or her turn, stating kindly that he'll ask another student and return to him or her later.

CLASSROOM EPISODE #6

> **K:** Well this guy is saying, "Look at me, look at me, look at me—I'm poison, you can't eat me." So he's advertising himself. He says, "I want to be sure you see me and I want to make sure you remember me very well, because remember you ate that bug last year and got real sick—well then don't eat me, you'll get sick again." So it's advertising itself. Which do you think then, is it camouflaging itself or is it advertising itself? (Long pause) I'll ask Sean, and then I'll come back to you. Sean, what do you think?

Ken's reflective comments (subject matter content):

> And I think it's important; a couple of the kids preferred not to take a guess, or not to take a chance. [A]And there's really no winning or losing in this, and there's no, it's not, your name isn't going to be written up on the board if you guess wrong. [B]A lot of these kids, and it may be with kids in general, but in this population in particular, really prefer not to take the chance. [C]And, as a result, they either (a) don't get that satisfaction of being right, but (b) more importantly, they don't have to think it through. And that's really the core of what I'm trying to get at. [D]So I always make sure, if the student says, "I don't really know, or I don't really want to guess," I say, "Well I'm going to come back to you, and then you can guess later because everybody's going to say what their idea is."

^EAnd sometimes I have to wait it out a long time, but it's worth the wait, because the next time that particular student is more willing to give their answer. And after a little bit of practice, they usually come up with more accurate guesses than from their original "I don't want to try."

Ken knows that his students need encouragement in order to actively participate in his instructional activities (B). However, he chooses not to force participation, but instead creates alternative opportunities (D) within a non-threatening environment (A), so that students can participate when *they* feel they are ready (E). Ken believes by doing so, his students will not only feel better about themselves but they will also have opportunities to think carefully about what he is trying to teach them (C), as opposed to just getting the "right" answer.

When Ken thinks about the subject matter he is going to teach, he does so in a way that reflects how he wants his students to think about that subject matter. It isn't the ability to recite the four reasons for insect coloration that is important, something other teachers might emphasize, but the ways in which his students can think about and use this subject matter content to understand the world around them that is central to Ken's teaching. Ken describes his approach to subject matter content as "the idea of thinking without being so explicit"—that is, the subject matter content is secondary to the value of having students think about and use that subject matter content in a context that is useful and meaningful.

To introduce the third reason why insects have color, mimicry, Ken places a brightly colored poster of what appear to be two monarch butterflies on the chalk rail. He asks the students to identify what type of butterflies these are and to think about why they might be so beautifully colored.

CLASSROOM EPISODE #7

K: So, now we move down to here, this is called—who knows what kind of butterfly this is? A lot of times we see it flying around.

S1: A monarch.

K: This is a monarch butterfly. Which of these two reasons do you think he's so brightly colored? Is it like that because it makes it easy to hide? If you ever see a monarch butterfly flying around, is it easy to see or hard to see; and then think about that and then decide which of those two reasons is a why monarch butterfly is so beautifully colored. I'm gonna ask everyone to give an idea, so everyone should think about it. (Ken circles the room asking each student, "Which do you think? Is it camouflaging itself, or is it advertising itself?") I'll give you a little hint. See that blue flower—now what do you think? Is it camouflaging itself on that blue flower, or is it really clear to see the monarch from the flower?

S1: Advertising.

K: So what do you think it is? Now put your hand up if you think it's camouflage. Put your hand up if you think it's advertising. Monarch butterflies taste awful. They taste so yucky, and they don't care whether anyone sees them or not. But this butterfly isn't a monarch (pointing to the second, smaller butterfly on the poster). This butterfly is called a viceroy butterfly, and he's sweet to eat. Why do you think he looks like that? Now think. This guy, monarch, is it sweet or yucky?

S2: Yucky.

K: Yucky. This guy is sweet. And I want you to look at those really carefully and decide, why did nature make this yummy, yummy, sweet-tasting butterfly almost look the same as that?

Ken's reflective comments (subject matter content):

And here again half the class had chosen "camouflage" and half the class had chosen "advertising;" I think it was about fifty-fifty. [A]I could have just said, "The monarch is brightly colored; it wants to advertise itself because it's a very bad-tasting insect." But, again, [B]I think it's important for kids to think it through in their own minds, and they pretty much have to reflect on their own experiences with seeing a monarch. So I wanted the kids who had guessed "camouflaging" to reflect on—even though I didn't say it—I wanted them to reflect on what it means to camouflage, and again, it's the idea about thinking without being so explicit. If camouflage is [C]"to blend in," is that blending in? And if the answer is "no," it's not camouflage. [D]Then, perhaps, the next time they come across a bug, they'll be able to think that same thing through, even if the teacher isn't there to say, [E]"Oh, that's camouflaging itself." Is it blending in? Yes; then that's camouflage. Is it blending? No; then there must be another reason."

When Ken reasons about how to present his subject matter content, he once again positions his approach as different from the traditional teacher (A), who might simply state the facts and expect the students to learn them. Instead, he reflects (B) on his underlying goal of getting his students to think for themselves, to relate what they already know to what they are learning, so that outside his classroom they might be able to think critically on their own about the world around them (D). Again we hear Ken take on the voices of his students (C and E), thinking and talking as they might as they engage in the sort of critical thinking Ken believes is essential for these students to succeed outside his classroom.

At what is now about the midpoint of the lesson, Ken shifts to a small group activity in which groups of three students will be expected to read a short passage from an article or a book about a particular insect and decide which of the four reasons explains why this particular insect has the coloration it does. Ken matches up the groups, giving each group one pencil, one piece of paper, and one copy of the reading. They get to work immediately, huddling around their readings, excitedly pointing at the pictures, making guesses as to why their insect has that coloration.

CLASSROOM EPISODE #8

K: Now I'm going to give each group of three kids something to read. Okay, Eddie, listen up for this. I'm going to give you some article or some part of a book to read, and most of the time what you have to do is guess what you're reading about—some kind of coloration on insects. Is it a camouflage thing? Is it an advertising thing? Is it mimicry? Or is it warning? Which of those reasons is why your bug is colored—or changes colors—the way it does?

Ken's reflective comments (appropriateness of teaching strategy):

[A]If this had been a mainstream classroom lesson, it probably would have been done in about half the time. And one of the important things that I find, partly, may even be a weakness with the way a lot of mainstream children are taught, is that there is not enough time to process the information. [B]There was a lot of repetition of the words, a lot of repetition of what they meant, slightly different explanations, slightly different descriptions. The words were read two or three times, pointed out, and probably now most of the kids—and we'll find out in the reading—most of the kids know what the four reasons are; they know there are four reasons. [C]Rather than saying, "There are four reasons why, the first one, the second one, the third one, the fourth one," talk a little bit about it and then go do something else. [D]So this takes a lot longer. But I think it also, especially for these kids, [E]it gets them thinking in this way, thinking in that way, going through the information in several different ways, reprocessing it, having to answer questions about it, going back, and in something that's mainly an oral presentation, I think it's really important to insure the comprehension by going at it from lots of different ways and having enough repeat time so that kids can process it all.

Ken justifies the appropriateness of this teaching strategy based on a combination of what he knows about his students' language skills and abilities, what he believes is important in language learning and teaching, and what he sees as weaknesses of the typical instructional model of schools. He compares what he has just done in this lesson (B) to what he believes occurs in most mainstream classrooms (A), once again taking on the voices of other teachers (C) so as to position himself against the traditional model of instruction—one that he believes is inappropriate for his ESL students. Ken characterizes his own teaching as taking more time, allowing for more in-depth processing of new information, and letting students discover for themselves rather than simply being told. All of this is necessary, Ken reasons, because of what he knows about his students' language skills and abilities and what he believes they need to become independent learners and users of the English language.

Many of Ken's decisions are based on his knowledge of his students' language skills and abilities. He anticipates that his students will have difficulty understanding the directions for this activity, so he quickly moves from group to group, asking each to restate the directions to make sure they understand what they are supposed to do. Once again, his questions force the students to think through what they are reading.

CLASSROOM EPISODE #9

K: Do you understand what you need to do from this? Can you tell me; can you use your own words, what . . . ?

S1: You have to go through page two, fourteen, eighteen, and twenty, and why are they so colorful?

K: Okay, and what do you have to write?

S1: Umm, umm.

K: Well, what do you have to write down on this?

S1: You have to write down things that they are.

K: Okay, use the words that I have here, "Write down"—what? What do you need to write down?

S1: Four reasons.

K: Well, what about the Hercules; are you going to write four reasons for that first beetle? How many . . . reason for what? The reason that what? Sean, what reason—the reason that. . . .

S2: How they'd get colorful?

S1: Why are they colorful?

K: The reason why it's colorful, and, your idea, why you choose that, either from the picture or from the text, which means from the words that go with it.

Ken's reflective comments (student language skill and ability):

[A]One of the things that kids seem to lose track of when they're reading directions is that all of the words go together as one idea. [B]So the directions say, "Write down what reason each is colored and why you think . . . ? So it's right there, you have to write down what reason you're choosing, and why you're choosing it. But they got what page they are supposed to be on, but the actual—you know there's really nothing inherently more difficult structurally about the question "Write down why," as opposed to "Read page . . . ," but you can skim or read carelessly, read page 2, but you still got the numbers and you say the word "read." But the other one, you have to think it through a little bit. And they had skimread the same way that they skimread the four page numbers and thought that they knew what they were supposed to do. [C]So that group could say what the directions were, but I want to further explore whether they actually have some organization for going about it. How are they going to figure that out, because none of the texts . . . , in a couple of cases it says it, but what are they going to look at to figure that out? Are they just going to be guessing? [D]And a lot of times I might find that they are guessing if they haven't had a chance to verbalize what they're going to do to figure it out.

Ken knows his students so well that he anticipates problems they will encounter (A), almost to the point that he reasons as they might reason (B); understanding the logic of their thinking and the reasons for their confusion (C). His strategy to head off potential problems is to provide a mechanism for his students to verbalize their understanding of an assignment or, in this case, the directions for a small group activity (D).

As Ken continues to monitor the groups' progress, he notices that one group appears confused. For this particular group the reading states two reasons why this insect has a given coloration, but scientists are only sure about one of those reasons. Ken asks the group a series of "or" questions to determine whether they have understood the reading.

CLASSROOM EPISODE #10

K: Advertising, but it might be two reasons, because it says it has a terrible taste, and it says it also has a tiny face. And then it says, "But nobody . . ." what does it say? Can anybody read that for me?

S1: "But nobody is really sure if this also helps protect it."

K: So, which one do you know it is? Is it the terrible taste—advertising—that this has, definitely? Or is it the funny-face warning? Which does it definitely have?

S2: The funny-face warning.

K: And read that again, Saddam; what does it say? "But nobody . . ."

S3: "But nobody is really sure . . ."

K: Does that mean they know or they don't know?

Ss: They don't know.

K: What don't they know?

S2: "They are not sure if this also helps protect . . ."

K: And what are they talking about, the face or the taste?

S1: The taste.

S2: The face.

K: Just look at the—well, which is it, Saddam?

S2: The face.

K: Okay, which are they sure about then? Are they sure about the terrible taste, or are they sure about the warning face?

S2: The warning face.

K: Read it again; read it again. Figure it out; figure it out.

Ken's reflective comments (appropriateness of teaching strategy):

[A]One kind of questioning that really confuses these kids a lot is an "or" question. Kids almost always chose the second part to say, you know, "Is it this or that," and they say "that" automatically, and [B]even though the words they had just read said "This insect has a terrible taste, it also has a face, but nobody knows for sure . . . ," so I said, "Now, which one do people know about, the terrible taste or the tiny face?" And, without losing a beat, they all said, "The tiny face." [C]And sometimes, well I often will deliberately, will put the answer part, the correct answer part, at the beginning, just to see if kids are really following the thought or whether they're just expecting the "[this or that . . . . It's <u>that</u>, that's right." [D]The way, you know, there's a common—especially in kindergarten—there's a questioning kind of style. [E]And you'll see that the second later I asked that question, and, without any thought at all, will say the wrong answer, even though they know it's not that.

Ken justifies (C) the appropriateness of his teaching strategy to intentionally trick this group to determine whether they are really thinking about what they have just read or whether they have based their answers on what they anticipate the answer will be. Ken explains this decision in terms of what he knows of his students' language skills and abilities (A), his knowledge of a typical teacher questioning pattern used in elementary schools (D), and his belief in the importance of getting students to think through what they are learning.

When Ken reaches the next group they are laughing and giggling about the fact that their insect, the leaf hopper, always jumps sideways. One of the group members doesn't seem to believe it, so the other two students point to the sentence in the reading where it says that leaf hoppers always jump sideways. Ken joins in on their excitement.

Classroom Episode #11

K: I took out tree hoppers because, in the one you're doing . . . right . . . about the world's weirdest bugs, there's a picture of a tree hopper. And, Phan, yesterday—

S1: Leaf hopper.

K: Excuse me, a leaf hopper. Did I say tree hopper? A leaf hopper, you're right. And Phan has a leaf hopper jumping around in there. A little tiny leaf hopper . . . remember, you saw that one?

S2: Jumping sideways.

K: Jumping all around. Tell everybody, what's strange, what's really bizarre about that leaf hopper?

S3: He jumps sideways.

K: And how did you learn that?

S3: In the book.

K: She learned it by reading. You don't have to learn stuff just because teachers tell you. You can learn stuff from the book. Did I tell you that, or did you read that from the words? Well what do you know? I bet you kids will learn a lot of stuff from the reading.

Ken's reflective comments (student affective needs):

> I figure that it's important to—they read something and they got that information on their own, and it's something they learned, they were quite happy about. [A]But I really wanted to emphasize that kids can learn on their own. They pick up a book, and they can read and they can learn stuff from it. [B]So, you know, just kind of like over-playing it, just so that everybody can get the sense of, "Oh gee, they learned something really neat, just by reading," [C]because I don't think they all have quite a sense that that's possible.

Ken's overly enthusiastic response to the group's discovery about leaf hoppers (B) was clearly done with consideration for his students' affective needs. Ken wants his students to feel good about themselves, but more importantly, he wants them to feel good about their ability to learn on their own (A), something he recognizes that many of them may not have.

Suddenly the bell rings and the students scatter in a semi-organized manner. They seem to know that chairs and tables must be returned to their original places and the papers, pencils, and readings must be returned to Ken before they leave the room. Ken shouts over the buzz that they will finish the readings tomorrow and then begin a coloring activity in which they will complete detailed drawings of the coloration of their insects.

Ken's reflective comments:

> It did take longer to do the reading, but there were more times than I thought that I had to actually refocus the kids on things that were actually in the print that they weren't picking up, either in the directions or the text. And, as I said at the beginning, I knew that these readings were a stretch for them, but armed with the information about coloration, I really wanted them to make that stretch and to really feel proud of themselves. These kids, they're always extremely proud of themselves when they really feel like they put in a good amount of time on something that's challenging. And, you know, I try to keep it as matter-of-fact and easygoing as I can and, then, when the work is done, we reflect on what a challenge it was. But, you know, "By golly we did it," and here we're going on to the next thing to keep them constantly moving forward. There is such inertia that's built in, and I think you can get the sense from watching how

much the inertia of not thinking things through really can take over, unless there's a constant pushing here and nudging here, pulling here, reminding . . .

Overall, Ken's reasoning is shaped by what he knows about his students, by his own beliefs about language learning and teaching, by his own image of himself as a teacher of these ESL students, and by what he knows of the traditional model of instruction found in schools. Each of these considerations factors into how he conceptualizes, develops explanations for, and responds to what occurs among his students in this classroom. Exploring the complex nature of Ken's reasoning in this way enables us to better understand why Ken teaches the way he does.

---

1 *REFLECTING ON REASONING TEACHING*

The following Investigation asks you to reflect on Ken's reasoning as a way for you to understand the complex nature of teachers' reasoning. It will also help you formulate a starting point from which you can begin to reflect on your own reasoning.

In your reflective journal or with other teachers:

A. What did you find to be the most striking feature of Ken's teaching? Why? How is Ken's teaching similar to or different from your teaching? If you were teaching this lesson, what would you have done differently? Why?

B. Reflect on Ken's comments about his own teaching. Do you think about similar things while you are teaching? How are your and Ken's interactive decision-making styles similar and/or different? Why do you think this is so?

C. Construct a concept map that visually depicts the complex nature of Ken's reasoning. Include all the factors that seem to shape his reasoning. How are they interconnected? What factors seem to figure more prominently than others? Speculate on why you think this is so.

---

2 *WHAT WORKS: REFLECTING ON EFFECTIVE LESSONS*

Teachers are extremely busy people and there is little if any time built into the teaching day to reflect on one's own teaching practices. However, if you take the time to reflect on your teaching practices you can gain insight into why you teach the way you do. More important, insights into your teaching can help you determine what you must consider when planning new lessons or managing other dilemmas that occur in your classroom.

A. In writing, describe one lesson you taught during the last week that you feel was very effective. Include descriptions of the following:

- The content and purpose of the lesson

- What you did during the lesson

- What the students did during the lesson

- What made the lesson effective (be as specific as possible)
- Why you believe this was an effective lesson (be as specific as possible)

B. With other teachers, share your descriptions of your lessons. Include the following:

- Provide an overview of the content and purpose of the lesson
- Describe what you and the students did during the lesson
- Describe what you believe made it an effective lesson

C. In writing, reflect on one new insight you gained from hearing about other teachers' effective lessons. Include the following:

- Describe one new insight you gained
- Describe how you plan to apply this new insight to your own teaching

---

3 *PEER MENTORING: LEARNING FROM OTHER TEACHERS*

While teachers can learn a great deal from one another, busy teaching schedules and the isolated nature of the teaching profession do little to encourage teachers to work and learn from one another on a daily basis. Peer mentoring programs are designed to create supportive, open relationships among teachers in which they can share their experiences, ideas, and concerns and learn from one another over an extended period of time.

Below are three examples of ways that peer mentors can work together. Each is designed to help you examine the intricacies of your own teaching through self-reflection, critical analysis, and individualized sense making.

A. With your peer mentor discuss and reflect on the following:

- How do you deal with a particular instructional consideration?
- How do your students respond?
- How successful are you at dealing with this instructional consideration?
- What might be some alternative ways of dealing with this instructional consideration?

B. Observe your peer mentor teach while taking note of one predetermined instructional consideration. After the observation reflect on the following:

- How did he or she deal with this instructional consideration?
- What would you have done if you were in his or her place?
- How might his or her instructional strategies be useful in your teaching context?

C. Select any of the Investigations in Chapters 6, 7, or 8. Complete one with your peer mentor.

---

4 *CONDUCTING INTERVIEWS ABOUT TEACHING*

If you are unable to observe other teachers, try conducting an interview with one or more teachers about how they deal with a particular instructional consideration. As you talk, take note of how teachers tend to "contextualize" their answers by saying that what they do during classroom instruction depends on a host of factors that are embedded in themselves, in their students, and in their classrooms.

A. Ask the teacher(s):

- How does he or she deal with a particular instructional consideration?

- Why does he or she deal with this instructional consideration in this particular way or ways?

- What might be some alternative ways of dealing with this instructional consideration?

B. Share your interview(s) with a classmate, a teacher, or your instructor.

- Discuss how the teacher(s) you interviewed dealt with the instructional consideration.

- Discuss what you learned from conducting interviews about teaching.

7

REASONING TEACHING IN A SECONDARY ESL PROGRAM

ANNE: MEETING STUDENTS' INDIVIDUAL NEEDS

Spend a few days in Anne's seventh- and eighth-grade ESL classroom and you realize right away that Anne is a "shoot from the hip" kind of teacher. She tells it like it is: with her students, with other teachers, and with anyone else who cares to listen. She has a loud gruff voice that grabs your attention as soon as you walk in the room. She laughs and jokes with the students as they mill around the room waiting for class to begin. She tells one student to "stash the hat." She asks another to "have a seat." She hands another a homework assignment and says sarcastically, "I think you finally got it!" But under her gruffness there is a sensitivity, a caring that Anne clearly feels deeply for each of her students. You see it in the way she smiles as the students tell her what they think about a particular character in the story they are reading. You see it as she patiently waits for students to collect their thoughts before speaking in front of the class. You hear it in her coaching voice that responds to students' claims of "I don't know" with "Sure you do—I know you do." She describes herself as

> a facilitator, as someone who's here to take the students and help them to know what their own abilities are, and to encourage them to go as far as they can with those abilities. Not as someone who has to teach a certain set curriculum or, I don't feel that there's a certain amount of material that has to be covered every year, or, if this lesson has to change due to something else, that's going to change things. I will feel badly if, at the end, the kids don't have more self-confidence, feel better about themselves, have more interest in different types of things, and be able to feel that next year they can do better.

Such genuineness is evident in all that Anne does for and with her students.

> I think my major strength is, I really like the kids. I genuinely like all of them, no matter how rotten they are. And I think they can sense that. Therefore, when they're having troubles, or when they've done something wrong, they know it's not because I picked on them personally, or that I don't like them, but because they've done something wrong. And because I have this affection for them, I also feel that it's easier for me to find out what is wrong sometimes.

Given the makeup of Anne's classes, you might say that she has some of the toughest cases in this large urban middle school. All of her students are learning English as a second language, but several of them have other, more serious learning disabilities. Some come out of tough ethnic neighborhoods and others have had traumatic experiences leaving their countries to emigrate to the United States. All are adolescents, and according to Anne, this age is tough for any kid, but it's particularly tough for these kids. She jokes that for some of these kids it's more important for them to learn how to play baseball than to memorize history facts. On top of the difficulties of this age group, there is the enormous amount of academic content that her students must be able to handle if they are to function in the regular seventh- and eighth-grade classes. Anne claims that that is the ultimate goal for these students:

> If they were in their own countries doing their own languages, they would be at a certain level. I would like them to be able to be at that level in this country. Before I'd move them out into the regular classrooms I consider things like their study habits, do they still need to be in small groups. We have some kids who, if I didn't call their parents once every two weeks to get them tuned in again, they would not be passing right now. Do they have any other learning problems? Can they write? A lot of them speak very well but can't read or write, or they don't get it unless you explain it to them a lot of different ways, so if I feel they can do regular classroom work without help, and do well, we'll move them out of here.

But moving her ESL students into the regular classroom is secondary to Anne's goal of building their self-confidence in themselves as students, as language learners, and as people. She credits this goal to a fellow teacher who was at one time her supervisor, but who later became head of the ESL department in her school.

> I had been teaching reading, and my supervisor was probably the best teacher I have ever seen in my life, and I learned most about what I know about teaching from watching her teach. She had a wonderful way with any student. It was obvious to any student that she was interested in them, liked them, understood them, and she could figure out a way to teach almost any student.

As a student herself, Anne was most affected by teachers who encouraged her to think for herself, who allowed her to pursue her own interests, and who were interested in what she had to say. Anne claims this carries over into her own teaching since she wants her students to think for themselves, explore their own interests, and have confidence in their own abilities as learners.

> I think often people who teach ESL think that they're teaching ESL as some separate item that has nothing to do with any other kind of learning. And the way I look at it is they're simply students who need to learn a new language and their brains are working just fine, and they can think very well. They have wonderful ideas, and they can do almost anything. It just needs to be explained a little more clearly to them.

Anne's ESL classes focus on academic content, both literature and social studies, and they count for legitimate academic credit within the school. So if students can function in Anne's content-based ESL classes, they will eventually be able to function in their regular content-area classes. But for Anne, her students are not just learning English, they are learning to believe in themselves.

ANNE: THE SUMMER OF THE SWANS

As the bell rings, the students are still milling around the room; most seem anxious about where to sit (there is a video camera in the room today), some are collecting their books and papers in preparation for today's ESL/literature class, others are talking quietly in small groups. After a few opening comments, Anne returns a grammar test they took on Friday. The test was on appropriate verb tense usage, something Anne says her students have enormous difficulty with in their writing. Anne explains:

> I've been going through the irregular past tense verbs with them, and we've already learned several other verb tenses. Now I'm mixing them up and trying to teach them how to do this by looking for clues. So that they can find the word—"did" or "could" or "may" or "'ing" or "is"—they'll know what goes with it. So that they will understand better what's the correct form of the verb to "put in."

There seems to be a familiar pattern to the way Anne goes over this test. The teacher-student exchanges are fast-paced round robin, and the students obviously know this routine well. As Anne moves from student to student, each reads a sentence and Anne asks the student to explain why he or she selected the verb tense. She then listens to the student's explanation and restates it with more details by emphasizing how the verb tense affects the overall meaning of the sentence. On the surface this appears to be a typical ESL grammar drill. However, for Anne this activity fulfills a different purpose: to provide these students with a strategy for figuring out appropriate verb tense usage on their own once they enter the regular classes.

CLASSROOM EPISODE #1

A: Then let's go through the sentences. I think all of you are getting a lot better on these sentences. Arthur, you did a whole lot better this time. You want to read the first one?

S1: (Students retrieve the paper from his desk) "Give him—"

A: No, the sentences down at the bottom, Arthur.

S1: Oh, "Will Michelle . . ."

A: Michael.

S1: "Will Michael light the candle at the seder?"

A: Seder . . . did you have a seder at Passover?

S1: What is it?

A: You know, at Passover time?

S1: What does *seder* mean?

A: Did you eat a special meal at Passover? That's called a seder, that meal that you ate. OK, now, why did you put *light*? For the verb there. What's the clue word in that sentence?

S1: Will.

A: Right, the word *will,* you just copy that word over again. Right, *will.* And what time frame are we talking about here? Did this happen already? Is it going to happen some time in the future? Is it happening right now?

S1: It's gonna happen at seder—later, not now, but at the seder.

A: Right, it hasn't happened yet, but it's going to happen at seder. How did you know when this was going to happen? What word clued you in?

S1: *Will.*

A: Right, Jonathan, how about the next one?

Anne's reflective comments (curriculum integration):

> [A]They are in a way doing metacognition. They're telling why they think this. [B]But after they no longer have ESL, they're going to have to have a way to figure out why they should do something, and [C]they are going to have to know something other than the right answer for this test, which is why we're doing this.

Anne's justification (B) for this instructional activity is based on the need to provide her students with learning strategies that will help them be successful learners outside the ESL classroom. For Anne, it's not the grammar test itself that is important, but (C) the "figuring out why" that will enable them to function successfully in the regular seventh- and eighth-grade curricula. Thus this instructional activity (A) is an attempt to simulate the kind of thinking Anne knows her students will need in the regular classroom.

After going over the grammar test, Anne reminds the class of a homework assignment in which they are to create two "spidergrams" that illustrate themes in the book *Summer of the Swans*. Knowing that her students need concrete models that explicitly show them what they are expected to do, Anne asks the class to help her construct an example of a spidergram on the board. Such models, Anne believes, are necessary if students are to "get the right idea," know what they are supposed to do, and have an opportunity to try it out before being expected to do it on their own.

CLASSROOM EPISODE #2

A: Now, for tomorrow—now, switch your brains around, we're finished with grammar, we're not doing that anymore, *Summer of the Swans,*—okay, back to *Summer of the Swans,*—you all thought about themes that are in that story—main ideas—I want you to pick two of them and make spidergrams. Now Masinori is new in this class, so he doesn't know what a spidergram is, I bet, and neither does Jonathan. So let's do one for him. Paulina, can you think of a theme that's in *Summer of the Swans*?

S1: Don't judge a book by its cover.

A: OK, let's make that shorter, "don't judge by appearances"? (Writes on board) OK, so here is the body of the spider (points to center circle), and spiders have a lot of legs (draws lines out from the center circle), don't they? As a matter of fact, how many legs do spiders have?

S1: Eight.

A: Eight, but you can have an imaginary spider with twenty legs on your spider if you want, so what's an example from this story of "don't judge by appearances"?

S1: When Sarah said that "If all people that look smart are smart?"

A: Okay, Sarah, "All people who look smart, are smart." Okay, who's got another example? Jonathan.

S2: She also said that if people are beautiful—if they look beautiful, they are beautiful. (Anne writes on the board.)

A: Okay, if you look beautiful, you are beautiful. What's another one?

S3: She judged, like Joe, she like, she said that he did it, she judged him. She thought that he stole Charlie's watch. She thought he was like a bad person.

A: And what was the appearance that she judged him on? What was the thing that happened that made her decide that?

S1: I don't know.

A: Sure you do. What did he do that made him look guilty?

S1: Gave back Charlie's watch.

A: Yeah, Joe gave back the watch, so she assumed that he stole it.

Anne's reflective comments (student language skill and ability):

> [A]So there, Deana had the right idea, but she really had no idea why it was the right idea. I'm not sure she really understood why she said what she said. [B]But almost everybody has the right idea, [C]if you can just get around to it.

Anne's knowledge of her students' abilities (A) is evident in how she responds to their attempts and how she encourages them to express themselves, even when their answers are not exactly what she is looking for. Anne has tremendous faith in her students' potential (B), even if this potential seems hidden at times. Her consideration of her students' language skills and abilities and her knowledge of adolescents fuel her faith in her students, and she views her role as bringing this potential to the surface (C).

After the class has constructed a fairly extensive spidergram on the board, Anne repeats the homework assignment, checking with individual students to make sure they know what they are supposed to do.

CLASSROOM EPISODE #3

> **A:** OK, so Masinori, do you understand what you have to do for tomorrow? How you have to do this? You have to pick two ideas or themes from the story—here's an example of a theme in the story—and think of as many things that happened in the story, that are examples of that idea, or theme. OK, so you can take one piece of paper, on one side of it put a big circle with one theme in the middle, and on the other side put the other theme, then think of as many things as you can. OK, you got that, Jonathan? Okay, now, so that's the homework. Has everybody written this down? And Arthur, did you write it down? Paulina, did you write it down? I wrote it down; I'm going to remember it.
>
> **S1:** I wrote it down.
>
> **A:** Masinori's got it written down; I can see that. Jonathan, did you write it down?
>
> **S2:** I wrote it in my head.
>
> **A:** Roman wrote it down.

Anne's reflective comments (student understanding):

> [A]If you noticed in this class, everything gets repeated four hundred and seventy-two times, and [B]there will be people who won't know what the homework is tomorrow. [C]And you write it down, you talk about it, you have them say it. You think of as many ways as you can to do the exact same thing and you just hope that most kids will get it.

Despite the tremendous faith Anne has in her students, she also knows the realities of working with adolescents (B). To ensure that her students understand exactly what is expected of them, Anne continually repeats every direction and every question, and even paraphrases the students' contributions to ensure student understanding (A). Further, Anne provides students with multiple channels and multiple opportunities to understand the content of her instruction (C).

Anne now shifts the lesson to a discussion of a short passage from *Summer of the Swans*. In this particular passage the author uses an analogy to illustrate a central theme in the book. Anne describes how the author compares life to a flight of uneven steps and, with a puzzled tone in her voice, asks the class what they think this means.

CLASSROOM EPISODE #4

A: Okay, we . . . once again, I'm going to read this one little thing where it says . . . about Sarah, and she's talking about life, and she says how it's like steps, uneven steps. And she says, "She suddenly saw life as a series of huge uneven steps. And she saw herself on the steps, standing motionless in her prison shirt, and she had just taken an enormous step out of the shadows and was standing waiting, and there were other steps in front of her, so that she could go as high as the sky." Now, we said they're uneven because . . . who had that great idea about that? Who did that? I think it was Sasha, but anyway, Roman? Why are her steps uneven?

S1: Because different parts last longer.

A: Last longer . . . maybe, okay, different parts of your life last longer.

S2: Different times of your life, like sometimes things go up at a certain time, some go down at a certain time. Sometimes we behave really good and sometimes we behave very bad. So, step down and step up.

A: So, life is harder at some times than others, okay. But now it says, she just took a step up.

S3: Her days are not the same.

A: Her days are not the same. That's for sure, are they?

S3: Yeah.

A: Now it says, "She just took an enormous step out of the shadows." What did she just do?

S4: She saved Charlie.

A: She just saved Charlie, that's for sure.

S5: She changed her appearance—outward, she's not the same anymore, so she's different.

A: OK, so she's changed her idea of her own self.

S6: Like, she'd gone out of some hard things and now she's going on to something else.

A: Yeah, she's starting a whole new—she knows it's new doesn't she, OK, Kev?

S4: Maybe she's not a child anymore, she's grown up

A: Yeah, do you believe it? Is it possible to grow up? (Laughs)

Anne's reflective comments (student language skill and ability):

> [A]So, we try to bring the story to their own personal lives as much as possible. [B]Kids, especially seventh grade, have a great deal of trouble with abstract thinking. And they're all at different levels there. [C]But that doesn't mean that you can't try to get them to see it somehow. I mean you still have to, I mean they're not going to learn to do it unless they keep being prodded toward doing it. And so [D]I've seen them improve with this kind of thinking as the year has gone on. And you just have to keep on with it.

One of the most obvious instructional considerations that consistently shapes Anne's reasoning is her knowledge of this particular age group, adolescents. It's clear that many of her decisions are based on what she believes adolescents can and can't do. Anne devotes a good deal of instructional time to a discussion of this analogy based on her knowledge of her students' language skills and abilities. Anne knows (B) her students struggle with abstract thinking, something she credits, in part, to their age. Yet it's also obvious (C) that she believes her students have the potential to think abstractly, and that it is somehow her responsibility as their teacher to make sure that they have opportunities to do so. Anne's choice of this instructional strategy (A), relating abstract ideas within this story to her student's own lives, has (D) already proven to have a positive impact on her students' abstract thinking skills. And, while not stated explicitly, it appears as though Anne believes such abstract thinking skills are essential if her students are to succeed outside her classroom in the content-area classes in the school.

The students actively contribute to the discussion; focusing on the symbolism of the stairs and how life and our experiences in life change how we see both the world around us and ourselves. Anne validates each student's contribution with a pattern of repeating what was said and then probing for further information with follow-up questions. When this pattern stumps one student, Anne waits patiently for the student to collect his or her thoughts before asking another student to offer his or her ideas.

CLASSROOM EPISODE #5

A: Now it says she was standing, waiting, and there were other steps in front of her, so she could go as high as the sky? What does that part mean about her? Jonathan, do you want to take this one?

S1: Yeah, I'll do that one, that she could go as high as the sky.

A: What does that mean for her? I mean, does that mean that she really can climb up to the sky?

S1: No, if she could climb up to the sky, she would climb up.

A: So what does it mean?

S1: That she thinks she's going to live forever.

A: Do you think—do you think that? Masinori, what do you think it means, she's going to live forever? What do you think it means?

S2: It means . . .

A: She can go as high as the sky. (long pause) She can go as high as the sky. Remember we talked the other day about the expression "the sky is the limit." What does it mean, "the sky is the limit?" Kevin, what does that mean?

S3: There no limit for how high you want to go.

A: There is no limit of how high you can go.

Anne's reflective comments (student affective needs):

> [A]Now he (S2) is new to the class, he is shy anyway, and now we have a video camera. [B]But, I had to give him time. I try to give them all as much time as possible, not rush to the next person. [C]But a way to save face for him was to kind of change the question, so that it's the same question, but someone else can now answer it for him.

While Anne wants her students to be actively engaged in her instruction, she also recognizes the affective needs of her students (A); particularly students who need more time to collect their thoughts (B), or who need a face-saving way out of answering a question for which they feel unprepared (C). Again, Anne's consideration for her students' affective needs is balanced with her goal of keeping her students motivated and involved in her instruction.

Anne moves to the next sentence in this passage, asking Arthur—a student with severe learning disabilities—to explain what he thinks this section of the passage means. As Arthur struggles to express himself, Anne walks him through his explanation, encouraging, coaxing, and probing a response out of him.

CLASSROOM EPISODE #6

A: Okay, now look at this one. She saw Charlie on a flight of small difficult steps. Where did she see Charlie?

S1: What's "flight of steps"?

A: Arthur, a flight of steps is a set of steps; to go from the first floor to the second floor is one flight. So, Arthur, what do you think? Why does she see Charlie on a flight of small difficult steps?

S1: I didn't get it.

A: Well, let's get it now. Why is Charlie having small difficult steps? (long pause) What do you know about Charlie?

S1: He can't talk.

A: That he can't talk. What else?

S1: He's kind of dumb or something.

A: Okay, so why is he having small difficult steps?

S1: He's mentally retarded.

Anne's reflective comments: (student language skill and ability):

> [A]I really like him (Arthur) and he knows it. I mean, I think that's important. [B]He's been diagnosed with attention deficit disorder and I know this is tough for him. With this book, [C]I read almost all of the first half of the story into a tape recorder for him, but after that he seemed to be able to do it. [D]Once he got into it, and understood what it was about and so forth, he was able to do it, but he couldn't do it at all before that. [E]I modify the work for him.

Anne's unshakable faith in her students' potential and her knowledge of their wide range of language skills and abilities become the justification for her decisions to modify her instruction to meet the individual needs of her students. It is obvious from Anne's comment (A) that she really cares about her students, and that this is not only important for her students and for learning, but also part of her image of herself as a teacher. Because she knows (B and D) that this student has been diagnosed with a learning disability and that many of her instructional activities will be difficult for him, she modifies her instruction in different ways (C and E) to enable him to succeed. Her comments remain consistent with her belief in the importance of constructing and modifying instructional activities to meet the individual needs of her students.

The discussion continues without missing a beat, as Anne continues soliciting comments from other students about this same passage from the story.

CLASSROOM EPISODE #7

S2: He can't do a lot of things, so in school they just treat him, I don't know, like he's dumb or something.

A: Okay, what about school, what did they . . . they said something about what he learned to do in school? Yeah.

S1: He learned how to write the alphabet.

A: But how is it for him to do it?

S1: It's very hard for him to do it. And because he has a brain damage, life is going to be harder than for like normal people, and he's going to have a difficulty. That's why he has like small steps.

A: Yeah. Do you agree, Kev?

S2: Everybody still treats him like a baby, like he is a baby, and he's kind of old.

A: He's being treated like someone who is much younger than he is.

S2: He's like, yeah, he needs more attention, more help. That's like how babies are too, they need more attention; they can't talk or do nothing.

Anne's reflective comments (student language skill and ability):

[A]You can see from watching the different kids comments on the same topic that some of them are very concrete and some of them are abstract. [B]But even Deana, she's very concrete, but she was helped to get to that thought by hearing the other people's comments.

Despite the fact that they are adolescents, Anne recognizes (A) that her students are at very different levels and therefore think very differently about the same topics. Thus she allows the students to freely share their ideas without correction or interruption based on her knowledge of their language skills and abilities. Yet she also recognizes (B) the instructional value of letting students share their ideas, regardless of how concrete or abstract they are, because such exchanges, Anne believes, help students broaden the ways in which they think about new ideas.

The discussion is really rolling now. Students begin to offer their ideas without being called on, talking directly to one another, commenting on each others' contributions instead of just responding to Anne. At one point Anne breaks in and asks one of the quieter students to comment on what was just said. Anne waits patiently for his response.

CLASSROOM EPISODE #8

A: This is the most interesting one, I think—she sees her father down at the bottom of some steps, just sitting and not trying to go further. What do you think about that one? The father is at the bottom, just sitting there and not trying to go more. Okay, Roman, what do you think about that?

S1: Because he like doesn't see them as much, and he's like is having the hardest times, because he has to like work all the time, and the only time he goes home is on weekends, because he has to get money for Sarah and Charlie to live on.

Anne's reflective comments (appropriateness of teaching strategy):

> [A]I waited a minute. Some kids had their hands up, but I didn't call on those kids. [B]A lot of times there are certain students who raise their hand immediately, and they really don't know what they're going to say; they just raise their hand. And, secondly, [C]I think, sometimes people don't raise their hands because they're not sure they can do it but they really can, if they try.

Besides modifying her instructional activities to meet the individual needs of her students, Anne also modifies her own instructional behavior in order to create opportunities for quieter students to participate in her instruction. At this point in the lesson, Anne considers (A) the appropriateness of her decision to interrupt the discussion and call on a quieter student. Yet she justifies (B) her decision, based on her knowledge of her students and her belief (C), once again, in the potential of all students, quiet or not.

As the discussion continues, it becomes clear that this passage represents the crux of the story, the central theme that Anne wants her students to recognize, a theme she hopes they will relate to their own lives and possibly see through the eyes of the characters in this story.

CLASSROOM EPISODE #9

A: Do you remember when she described the picture of her dad a long time ago, when she was little—a picture with her?

S1: Yeah.

A: What did it look like when her mother was still alive, when his wife was still alive? What did that picture of her look like? Would you sit up please? Yeah?

S2: He was happy, because we have like the smiling.

A: And what's he like now when he comes home? Arthur, what's he like now? When he comes home on weekends, what does he do?

S3: He watch TV, he stays on the couch.

A: Yeah, does he talk to the kids?

S3: No, he's just like . . . and the kids is thinking, "Why did you came here for, just to watch TV?"

A: Yeah, why did you bother to come home? So, yeah, what does that tell you about him? Something has happened to him.

S3: He watches TV in the house.

A: Right, so what has happened to him between the time he used to be the happy smiling dad and now when he just comes home and doesn't even talk to anybody? Kev?

S3: Too much stress.

A: Too much stress? OK.

S4: Tired.

A: Tired.

S3: Exhausted.

A: Exhausted, what else?

S5: Annoyed with his life.

A: Annoyed with his life?

Anne's reflective comments (student understanding):

> [A]They really don't get this, and a lot of it is because they're not adults, and they don't look at the problems from an adult's point of view. They know the facts, but they can't put themselves in his shoes and imagine what he must feel like. [B]So, I went back to something in the story which shows more what he feels like.

Anne describes her decision to return the students' attention to a critical incident in the story to ensure student understanding. Again, Anne admits (A) that her students are having difficulty understanding the central theme in this story because of their age and the difficulties they have thinking abstractly, yet she continues (B) to reinforce these skills by asking them to reflect on how the characters in the story might be thinking or feeling. It is this bridge between the students' own lives and the abstract ideas embedded in this story that Anne hopes this lengthy in-class discussion will help construct for her students.

The discussion winds down and with the few minutes remaining in the period, Anne asks the students if anyone would be willing to share their "Ugly Duckling" stories. These are stories they have been working on over the course of this literature unit, in which they were to compare the central theme in the children's story *The Ugly Duckling* to the central theme in *Summer of the Swans*. Anne calls on a very softspoken student.

CLASSROOM EPISODE #10

A: Masinori, why don't you read yours? That was—you did a good job on that, Arthur. Yeah, go ahead.

S1: *The Ugly Duckling.* When the swan was a young bird, the swan thought he was ugly, because everyone thinks he's ugly. He was ugly, and everyone made fun of him—about his looks. But, in the story, the main character, Sarah, thought she was ugly.

A: What else did you write?

S1: And, one summer when Charlie disappeared, she changed because she noticed that there were more important things than the things she used to care about.

A: Very interesting idea. There were more important things than what she used to care about. What did she decide was more important?

S2: Not just looks.

Anne's reflective comments (student language skill and ability):

[A]So, he actually had the whole story right; he did it right. [B]He had the simple ideas right. [C]But he started off being very nervous, so we couldn't understand anything . . . had to get him stopped—started again, and [D]then he really did all right.

Anne is unashamedly proud (A) when this student actually reconstructs the story through somewhat simple ideas (B) but clearly reflects abstract thinking. She recognizes what a struggle it was for this student to complete the task (C) but, given the time to think through his ideas and express them on his own terms, he was able to successfully retell the story (D).

The bell rings and the students begin to fidget in their seats. Yet they wait until Anne has reminded them of the homework assignment and praised them for the lively discussion they had today. She beams with pride as she glances around the room describing how difficult this story seemed at the beginning, but how everyone seemed to learn something about him or her self from reading the story. Several of the students smile back at her, embarrassed that she has brought attention to them but appearing proud just the same. When she finally dismisses the class, the students scramble around the room while Anne calmly collects her things and gets ready for the next class period.

Despite recognizing the limitations of this particular age group, Anne maintains a tremendous amount of faith in her students' potential to develop their abstract thinking skills and, ultimately, their overall abilities as learners. In Anne's final comment, she speaks almost passionately about her belief that each and every one of her students has the ability to learn.

Anne's reflective comments:

You can see that they can do it. [A]Just by the fact that they don't want to raise their hand or they're speaking so softly you can't hear it, or the fact that they can't express what they want to, [B]and I really—I believe they can all do it. I truly believe that there isn't anybody in the class who can't do the work that I've assigned, if they work harder, if they get help, or if they just want to. [C]And, so, they're different, each student has a different way to get at them. Some of them just don't do much work, and others have a lot of trouble and need to do more, some learn, they learn different ways, too, so that, [D]you just have to figure what it is that each person needs and try to give them that. But I really do believe they can all do it.

Anne recognizes (A) that some of her students lack the English language proficiency and/or motivation to do her assigned work on their own, but she also firmly believes (B) in her students' potential, that despite (C) individual differences every one of them can learn. Embedded in these beliefs we find (D) Anne's image of herself as a teacher: someone who must identify the individual strengths and weaknesses of each individual student and organize instruction around those strengths and weaknesses. Meeting the individual needs of her students appears to be an underlying goal of Anne's instruction.

Obviously, Anne's reasoning is shaped by her knowledge of this particular age group as well as by her knowledge of her students' individual needs, by an image of herself as a teacher who must meet those individual needs, by her knowledge of the skills and competencies her students will need to function outside her ESL classroom, and by her firm belief in the potential in all students. Each of these considerations factors into how Anne conceptualizes, develops explanations for, and responds to these students, in this classroom, in this school. Through this lens, we come to understand the complex nature of Anne's reasoning and better understand why she teaches the way she does.

---

1 *REFLECTING ON REASONING TEACHING*

The following Investigation asks you to reflect on Anne's reasoning as a way for you to understand the complex nature of teachers' reasoning. It will also help you formulate a starting point from which you can begin to reflect on your own reasoning.

In your reflective journal or with other teachers:

A. What did you find to be the most striking feature of Anne's teaching? Why? How is Anne's teaching similar to or different from your teaching? If you were teaching this lesson, what would you have done differently? Why?

B. Reflect on Anne's comments about her own teaching. Do you think about similar things while you are teaching? How are your and Anne's interactive decision-making styles similar and/or different? Why do you think this is so?

C. Construct a concept map that visually depicts the complex nature of Anne's reasoning. Include all the factors that seem to shape her reasoning. How are they interconnected? What factors seem to figure more prominently than others? Speculate on why you think this is so.

---

2 *WHAT I PLANNED—WHAT I DID: REFLECTING ON LESSON PLANNING*

Novice teachers often believe that if their lesson plans are not carried out, then their lessons have failed. This Investigation provides an opportunity for you to understand the relationship between the process of planning and teaching. In addition, it highlights how and why teachers deviate from their predetermined plans while teaching.

A. Prior to teaching a designated lesson, complete a prelesson planning guide in which you respond to specific questions related to a variety of instructional issues (see Lesson Planning Reflection Questions below).

B. Immediately after the lesson, complete a postlesson planning guide in which you respond to the same instructional issues, but this time by recalling what actually happened during the lesson.

C. Prior to your next scheduled teachers' meeting, complete a one-page written retrospective in which you focus on the differences and similarities between what you planned and what you actually did during this lesson.

D. During your teachers' meeting,

- describe the differences between what you planned and what you did;

- discuss your reasons for altering your pre-planned activities;

- discuss what you might do differently if you were to have an opportunity to teach the lesson again.

LESSON PLANNING REFLECTION QUESTIONS

Instructional Issues

Objectives

1. What will students take away from today's lesson?
2. What skills is this an occasion to teach, and how will students transfer these skills to future lessons?
3. What information should they retain from today's lesson?

Organization

1. How does this lesson follow from previous lessons?
2. How are the skills and information in this lesson connected to tomorrow's lesson?

Motivation/Engagement

1. Why should the students care about these skills or materials?
2. How can I motivate or interest them in the material?

Scaffolding

1. What prior knowledge can I draw on to help explain new material?
2. How can I help students make connections between new information and prior knowledge?
3. What about today's lesson will be most difficult for students?
4. What skills, tips, and structure can I give students to help them troubleshoot their difficulties?

Presentation

1. How will I order the presentation of information?

2. How can I ensure that the students understand my directions?

3. How can I make my expectations clear to the students? Will they know what to hand in?

Assessment

1. How will I know if the students master skills and important information outlined in my objectives?

2. How will I grade their products?

3 WHAT DOESN'T WORK: REFLECTING ON INEFFECTIVE LESSONS

This Investigation asks you to reflect on your teaching practices so that you can gain insight into why you teach the way you do. Reflecting on ineffective lessons can tell you a great deal about what you must consider when planning new lessons or managing other dilemmas that occur in your classroom.

A. In writing, describe one lesson you taught during the past week that you feel was ineffective. Include descriptions of the following:

- The content and purpose of the lesson

- What you did during the lesson

- What the students did during the lesson

- What made the lesson ineffective (be as specific as possible)

- Why you believe this was an ineffective lesson (be as specific as possible)

B. In small groups, share your descriptions. Include the following:

- Provide an overview of the content and purpose of the lesson

- Describe what you and the students did during the lesson

- Describe what made the lesson ineffective and why you believe it was an ineffective lesson

C. In writing, reflect on one new insight you gained from hearing about other teachers' ineffective lessons. Include the following:

- Describe one new insight you gained from hearing about other teachers' ineffective lessons

- Describe how you plan to apply this new insight into your own teaching

4 *Exploring Students' Perceptions of Your Teaching*

All too often, teachers make false assumptions about what their students are learning. Unfortunately, the only systematic feedback teachers tend to get from students, if any, comes at the end of a course or term. By making a regular habit of gathering feedback from your students about a particular activity or series of activities, you can better understand your students' perceptions of your teaching and tailor your instructional activities to better meet their needs.

After completing an activity or series of activities, ask your students to answer the following questions. Explain that you are interested in their honest feedback so that you can best meet their needs as learners and still fulfill the instructional objectives of the class. Explicitly state that their responses will not be graded, nor will they affect their grades. With young children, you may want to ask the questions orally in small groups. With older children and adults, the questions can be answered in writing.

A. Ask students to respond to the following:

Instructional Activities:

- I feel I gained the most from . . .
- I feel I gained the least from . . .
- The ideas/information covered would have been easier to understand if . . .
- I continue to have concerns about . . .
- If we were to do these activities again, I would like . . .

B. Each time you collect feedback from your students, write up a one-page summary of their responses and share it with other teachers or your instructor.

C. At the end of the course or academic term, reread your summaries and reflect on the following:

- What did you learn from gathering student feedback?
- In what ways did/will your teaching change as a result of gathering student feedback?

8

REASONING TEACHING IN AN INTENSIVE ENGLISH PROGRAM

ELIZABETH: ENABLING STUDENTS TO SUCCEED

The majority of Elizabeth's ESL students are enrolled in classes at the Intensive English Language Program (IEP) because they want to study at American universities. There are a few exceptions, such as the spouse of a graduate student who simply wants to learn conversational English, or a few students who are in the United States for a year in a study abroad program. But most intend to apply to an American university; need to obtain a minimum 550 TOEFL score; and must acquire the basic reading, writing, speaking, and listening skills that will be required of them as entering students. This goal weighs heavy on Elizabeth's shoulders. She speaks with concern about what will be expected of her students once they leave her classroom, and of the need for them to fit in and have the necessary academic skills to succeed in their university courses. But most importantly, Elizabeth knows they will be on their own.

> I try to teach my students the skills that they're going to need to succeed in the university and in the community by themselves, without me. I know that once they leave the classroom, they're not going to be able to rely on me or on other teachers. They're going to have to be able to do these things themselves. So I try to give them opportunities to practice on each other. I try to maintain a student-centered classroom, for the most part. I try to include the students in decision making whenever possible, and make them realize that they're responsible for their own learning, that they're not just going to be sitting there and hearing from me. That they need to participate actively in their learning.

Elizabeth describes her classroom as a "safe haven" for ESL students. The class sizes are small, usually between eight and twelve students, but never more than fifteen. The students spend all day in English language classes, rotating among teachers, but for the most part remaining as an intact group placed together based on their initial proficiency scores. This, Elizabeth says, makes them a "tight-knit group": they study together, eat together, and often socialize together. In Elizabeth's classroom and in the IEP in general, they are able to make new friends in a strange land and are surrounded by built-in support systems designed to help them succeed. Elizabeth describes the university outside her classroom as a "massive place." She knows many of the courses they will eventually enroll in will be large lecture sections of 500 or more students. No one will ask them if they have questions. No one will help them figure out complicated directions for assignments. No one will ask them what they think. They will be responsible for their own learning and their own success. Preparing her students for the university seems to permeate Elizabeth's image of herself as an effective teacher.

> An effective teacher is one who teaches skills rather than knowledge, so that the students can be successful on their own. Students should have a sense of their own autonomy and their own responsibility. They shouldn't feel dependent on the teacher completely. This doesn't mean that the students run the classroom. It means that they should feel they have some input into their own learning.

Elizabeth's goal of enabling students to succeed on their own also acts as the justification for the way she structures her instructional activities. Most of her activities require students to take responsibility for their own learning by being actively engaged in simultaneously using and learning the English language. At times this can cause problems because ESL students often have very different expectations about what a teacher should and shouldn't do in the classroom. Elizabeth acknowledges:

> People from different cultures come with different expectations of what's going to happen in the classroom. For example, some students think that the most important thing is for the teacher to correct their grammar. They're used to teacher-centered classrooms. They don't understand, sometimes, the value in student-centered teaching methods. So one of the difficult and most important aspects is being able to convince the students, to educate them, to make them understand that these are valuable exercises.

Not only must Elizabeth struggle with getting her students to actively engage in language learning activities, she must also convince them that her methods of instruction (student-centered, active participation) will eventually enable them to function in the world waiting for them outside the IEP. This is also difficult to do since even within one class there is a range of proficiency levels among students.

> This class is supposed to be an academic seminar. It's a high level, the highest level that we have in the IECP, yet we really have a mixed level class. We have some students whose English proficiency is quite high, while other students, because of their TOEFL scores or because of having lived in the United States for a while, were put into this highest level, but really aren't able to keep up with the work. Their listening comprehension isn't good enough really to be at this level, or their reading comprehension, and that makes it a little bit difficult when you're working with a class. I tend to aim a little bit at the higher level than at the lower level, because it's supposed to be a high-level class, so I feel that it's fair to aim at the higher level and then to try to compensate for these people who are at a little lower level with more one-on-one work and just a little bit of extra help.

While it may appear that Elizabeth carries much of the burden for enabling her students to succeed on their own, she also believes that the students' own motivation for learning English is essential for success.

> I think motivation plays a big part in learning languages. Whatever your motivation can be, it could be that you're in a foreign country and you need the language to communicate with the society, to fit in with the society. It could be that your husband speaks that language. It could be that you just like learning languages. It could be that you're planning to travel. It doesn't matter, as long as you have motivation. If you don't have any motivation to learn, I think it's difficult.

Such motivation lies at the heart of who Elizabeth is as a second language learner, since she credits her abilities to speak French, Korean, and some Russian and Swedish to her own internal motivation to learn other languages. She recalls learning Korean by

> going out into the markets and trying out what little Korean I had and people really appreciated that I was trying to speak their language. And that helped me, it helped to motivate me. And also my feeling that when you're in a country, you should do everything that you can to accommodate to the people who are there and not expect them to speak your language. So I tried as much as I could and I learned enough to get by and to communicate simply with them.

Besides her own internal desire to learn other languages, Elizabeth also credits her former teachers as having a tremendous influence on her as a second language learner.

> I think that the most influential thing for me as a second language learner was the teachers. For me personally it matters a lot whether I have a teacher who cares about teaching, who clearly cares about whether the student learns something, who clearly puts effort into making the class interesting. For example, I had a Swedish teacher in college, she was very sweet, very fun, exciting, she made the class exciting, she also created a very supportive atmosphere, so we had a combination of a very stimulating class with also a very supportive atmosphere. And it really motivated students to learn—not only myself, but everyone in the class.

The combination of both internal self-motivation and external motivation from her former teachers continues to shape Elizabeth's conception of herself as a teacher. She describes her teaching as student-centered, but to Elizabeth this means more than simply having students actively engaged in activities that are meaningful to them. Instead, she, as the teacher, always tries to envision her instructional activities through the eyes of her students.

> Second languages should be taught with the learner in mind and you should always keep in mind your own experiences as a learner. Try to put yourself in the place of the students. Try to think about how they're going to see this activity. What is important to explain to them; are they going to understand that this is an important or

a useful activity. Are they going to—what are they going to get out of this activity? Is this going to be something they will find scary?

Elizabeth tries to create a stimulating atmosphere for learning that will motivate her students to do their best by being sensitive to and aware of how to make the most of her students' diverse backgrounds and experience and by helping them take responsibility for their own language learning. Elizabeth claims that she tries to constantly evaluate her own teaching and use feedback from her students to continually improve her teaching. She sees herself as one who must enable her students to succeed on their own. She takes this responsibility seriously and so do her students.

ELIZABETH: TEACHING ACADEMIC READING SKILLS

Today's lesson is on developing academic reading skills, specifically, scanning texts for certain information. Elizabeth acknowledges that most of her students simply translate word-for-word entire texts, and given what she knows about university-level courses, she worries that they will never be able to keep up with the enormous amount of required reading material. Scanning is one useful reading strategy she believes will help them cope with the sheer quantity of reading material in their university-level courses. However, this approach to academic reading isn't an easy sell. Most of her students prefer to read every word or, as Elizabeth puts it, "for their own peace of mind, just to make sure they haven't missed something regardless of how long it may take them to do it their way."

Today's lesson is an opportunity for her students to practice scanning a text to look for specific information. The passage, entitled "Beware of the Dirty Seas," was taken from the British newspaper *The Observer*. Elizabeth begins the class by reviewing the concept of scanning and describing what she likes about the particular textbook in which she found this reading passage.

CLASSROOM EPISODE #1

E: Okay, we're going to move on to something a little different this second half of the class, although it relates to what we've been doing in the last couple of weeks and particularly to our subject from this morning. It's a reading skills exercise that comes from this book, which is called *Effective Reading*. It has a lot of reading skills exercises that I really like; I think they're very effective. You'll get some practice with scanning . . . . Does anyone remember what scanning is?

S1: Just to get the main thing, the main idea in one sentence from the paragraph, looking for—

E: Looking for?

S2: Highlights from the reading.

E: OK, that's when you skim, when you read very generally, just to get the main point, in scanning, you are looking for specific information.

S3: Like a specific name or day.

E: Right, like a specific name or day or a specific question that you are given, so you go through very quickly and find those particular points; you don't read all the words or all the sentences. We talked a little about this before, so we'll be coming back to that now.

Elizabeth's reflective comments (student motivation and involvement):

This particular book I really like. And I find that when I prepare the students very enthusiastically, they are generally more receptive to the materials and they approach it with a positive attitude, more positive than if I weren't enthusiastic or if I didn't tell them how much I like these materials. So I think that's a good way to start out the lesson.

Elizabeth then writes the title of the article, "Beware of the Dirty Seas," on the board. She asks the class to predict what they think this article will be about. Without prompts from her, the students call out their predictions.

CLASSROOM EPISODE #2

E: If you look at this title, "Beware of the Dirty Seas," what would you expect to read about?

S1: Pollution.

S2: Dirty Sea.

E: Dirty Sea, ha, yeah. What else? What about specifics?

S3: Maybe oil spills in the ocean.

E: Oil spills, yeah. What else? What else can cause pollution?

S2: Dead fishes.

S4: Industrial pollution.

S5: Sunken ships.

E: OK, yeah, all these things can pollute the seas.

S6: Yeah. One of the largest oil fields in the world we have in Venezuela now, and it's located in the lake. And its operations are over the lake of course. Inside the lake there are a complex mix of pipelines and valves, and every day there is a spill of oil. Even the oil companies try to take care of the spill, every day we have . . . and it's completely contaminated. We can't use the beaches, we can't use the walks, for instance.

This student's description of the pollution problems in Venezuela seems to prompt the other students to want to share their own stories. A Japanese student describes an incident in Japan in which people got sick from eating contaminated fish. A Turkish student describes the problem of industrial pollution in the rivers in Turkey. A Thai student describes a power plant located near a river that is polluting the main water source for thousands of people in his country. All of these contributions are spontaneous—in fact, Elizabeth simply nods her head with a distressed sort of look on her face. At this point in the lesson, everyone is engaged. They all seem to share a genuine concern for the environment and, somehow, their common concern seems to make the reading of this passage much more important.

Throughout this particular lesson, Elizabeth consistently creates opportunities for students to share their knowledge and expertise with one another. Often she does this with consideration for student motivation and involvement in the lesson. In Classroom Episode #2, she patiently allows each student to spontaneously share stories about incidence of pollution in his or her country.

Elizabeth's reflective comments (student motivation and involvement):

> [A]This is a chance for the students to share with each other and to share information about their countries. We've been talking about this particular topic in class for the past couple of weeks. This is another chance for them to develop their ideas and to share information from their own countries.

As her students provide graphic details of serious pollution problems in their countries, the class seems to share a genuine interest in and concern for the global environment. For Elizabeth, (A) having students develop their ideas and share information with one another remains consistent with her belief in the value of enabling students to learn from one another.

With the stage set for the scanning activity, Elizabeth reviews the directions for the first part of the activity. As the students begin to scan their texts, Elizabeth circulates around the room, making herself available for questions but not intruding upon their personal space unless invited.

CLASSROOM EPISODE #3

> **E:** In the first exercise we are going to be scanning, so don't read the whole text, only the information they ask for. You might find some words that you don't know—that's OK, don't run to your dictionary, only if you think the word is really important. Reading for specific information. Okay, the following passage is about pollution in the Mediterranean. Imagine that you're planning a holiday on the Mediterranean coast. Read the passage through, and note down the names of the places that you would be advised to avoid . . . to avoid, not to go there. Just underline or circle all those places that you think you should avoid, according to the author's information.

Elizabeth's reflective comments (student understanding):

> [A]I'm just checking to make sure that everybody understood the directions all right. They seem to have just got right to work, but I'm just checking to make sure that they understood, and, in fact,

^Bone student was reading through the whole article. ^CSo I tried to make it clear that he didn't need to read the whole article, but just look for those specific points in the reading.

Elizabeth continually monitors her students' actions to ensure student understanding. Knowing that her students tend to read word-for-word or, as Elizabeth put it, "to do it their way," she circles the room, checking to make sure that everyone knows exactly what they are supposed to do (A). When she discovers that one student is reading word-for-word (B), she reiterates her initial directions, emphasizing that the whole purpose of scanning is to gather specific information and not read the entire text (C).

There is silence in the room for about five minutes. While most of the students still seem engrossed in the reading, Elizabeth calls for their attention and asks about the places the author of the passage says should be avoided.

CLASSROOM EPISODE #4

S1: Israeli coast, Lebanon coast, Turkey coast, Syria coast . . .

E: Okay, you've jumped around, you've lost me a little bit— Israeli/Lebanon coast, and you also said . . . ?

S1: Turkey coast, Syria, and Lebanon.

E: Turkish coast.

S2: Israel.

S3: Syria and Turkey.

E: Syria and Turkey? I'm sorry, I didn't find anything about Turkey.

S4: There is no mention of Turkey.

E: Did I miss that? We've got the Israel/Lebanon coast, and okay, between Barcelona and Genoa. . . .

Elizabeth's reflective comments (appropriateness of teaching strategy):

So we're going back over the places that he had mentioned, and ^AI'm trying to get the students to find out whether the Turkish Coast was mentioned ^Brather than give them the answer or to say for sure that this was one way or the other. ^CI just ask them, "Did I miss that? I don't remember it being there, but maybe I missed it." ^DSo I give them a chance to find out for themselves.

There is nothing haphazard about Elizabeth's choice of teaching strategies. Given her belief in the importance of enabling students to succeed on their own (D), she intentionally uses teaching strategies that create opportunities for her students to identify their own errors (A). She knows she could easily tell them the correct answer (B), something that a more traditional language teacher might do; however, she prefers to take on the role of questioning reader (C), pretending she missed the information, so that her students must seek out the information for themselves.

After Elizabeth seems satisfied that they have identified all the places the passage suggested to avoid, one student jokes that they should cancel their trip, since there is no place they can go that isn't polluted. The class bursts into laughter and Elizabeth begins her introduction to the second scanning activity. In this activity, groups of three students will scan the passage looking for figures, numbers, and statistics that answer a list of questions given at the end of the passage.

CLASSROOM EPISODE #5

E: Okay, let's go on to the next one. It's a little more difficult. It requires a little bit more research. It's another scanning exercise, but now you're going to be looking for figures, for a mass, for numbers. Sometimes you'll find this in textual form, and you'll have to translate it into a number.

Elizabeth's reflective comments (appropriateness of teaching strategy):

[A]I'm having them work in groups for this particular exercise because it's a little more difficult and usually requires some discussion, and [B]they can really help each other. The last exercise was fairly simple in what it asked them to do, but this one requires a bit more analysis, a little more discussion. [C]It's a little more difficult for them, and [D]it can engender some good discussion in groups.

Knowing the complexity of this task (A and C), Elizabeth describes why she decided to have her students work in groups. Again her decision seems to recognize the competing demands of enabling her students to complete a complicated reading task while (B) at the same time creating an opportunity for them to learn from one another and (D) actively participate in their own learning. Not only is this group activity designed to create opportunities for students to learn from one another; it is, in Elizabeth's mind, an appropriate instructional approach for dealing with complicated tasks, such as scanning a technical reading. Active participation through meaningful student-centered interactions rests at the heart of Elizabeth's instructional practices. Such learning experiences in her classroom, Elizabeth believes, will enable her students to function successfully outside her classroom as well.

Elizabeth circles the room, making sure the groups know what they are supposed to do, stopping now and then to answer questions or to ask the groups to clarify their answers. Everyone is involved; the groups alternate from quietly scanning their texts to actively talking about tidbits of information they found. Elizabeth wanders over to a group seated in the middle of the room whose members appear to be working individually. Elizabeth waits patiently until a student acknowledges her with a puzzled look on his face.

CLASSROOM EPISODE #6

E: Do you have a question?

S1: No, we do it alone.

E: You decided to work alone?

S1: Yeah, alone first and then later look together.

E: OK, so you'll scan the reading on your own and then compare answers? That sounds like a good strategy. Is everyone OK with that?

S2: Yeah.

E: OK. But make sure you share your answers because you can learn a lot from each other and a lot of the information in this reading is not directly stated, it's implied, it's indirect, you have to figure out what they author means, or implies, because sometimes it's not directly stated. So make sure you check with one another.

Elizabeth's reflective comments (instructional management):

[A]This particular group, the middle group, they have decided that they would like to work separately, and then get together and compare their answers, and I agreed with that. I said that would be okay at this point. [B]I just wanted to remind them that it's really better if they work together because it gives them a chance to discuss and find the answers together. [C]But sometimes they think that they can go much faster on their own so they kind of abandon the rest of the group and it ends up just being an individual effort. Which is fine sometimes, [D]but I want them to realize the value of working together, particularly with this reading, where the author often stated things indirectly. [E]They'll have all the time in the world to work on their own once they leave my classes, [F]but for now I want them to use each other as resources, to learn from one another, to realize that this is a useful learning strategy.

Elizabeth's decision to interrupt this group was made with consideration for maintaining instructional management, because in her mind, (B) this activity was to consist of students working together to find specific information in the passage. And while she knows (C) that her students prefer to work on their own, she uses this as an opportunity to emphasize (D) why she wants them to work together and (F) to reiterate the instructional value of group activities. Indirectly, she seems to contrast (E) her own instructional activities (small groups) with the kinds of instructional activities she knows her students are likely to experience in the university (lecture). While it's obvious that Elizabeth believes there is tremendous value in having students share their knowledge and expertise with one another, her students don't always seem to recognize these as valuable learning opportunities.

As the groups begin to show signs that they are finished, Elizabeth announces that they will now go over the answers. She quickly reviews the answers for the remaining questions and then, returning to her original question, asks the class members to imagine that they are planning a trip to the Mediterranean, and based on the information they have just scanned from the passage, where they would go and what they would do.

CLASSROOM EPISODE #7

E: OK, good job. I'd really like to finish this exercise, maybe we'll finish this on Friday, but just to finish, I'd like to ask you a few questions. Now that you have a little bit of information about the Mediterranean, about the pollution there, if you were planning a trip to go there, what would you do, based on the information that you have from this passage?

S1: Don't eat fish.

E: Don't eat the fish.

S2: Don't swim.

E: Don't swim.

S3: Don't drink water.

S4: Don't go there.

S5: Don't drink the water from the faucet.

E: Don't drink the water from the faucet. Well, don't you think there's no reason to go there if you can't do those things?

S5: If you can't drink, if you can't swim, if you can't eat.

S6: What will I do?

S7: Some place doesn't matter for the swim. Some place for the sightseeing, for the architecture, for the building, or whatever, you know.

Elizabeth's reflective comments (student motivation and involvement):

Just to bring some closure to the class and to the parts of the exercises that we've been working on, [A]I decided to ask a few questions—opinion questions to the students—to get them thinking about their own ideas with relation to the article and because this is a nice way to end the class. [B]The students enjoy talking about their own experiences and bringing in their own knowledge to play in the discussion, and it's just a nice way of ending up.

At the close of this activity, Elizabeth decides to ask the students to relate what they have learned about the Mediterranean coast to their own lives (A). It seems obvious that this scanning activity isn't just an academic reading task. For Elizabeth it's a chance for students to gain new knowledge by scanning a complicated reading passage, but it's also a chance for students to share their own ideas and opinions about that new knowledge, and to enjoy themselves as well (B).

Other students begin to chime in, claiming there is more to most Mediterranean countries than their beaches. Elizabeth offers the floor to a student who mentioned that he was planning a trip to Spain.

CLASSROOM EPISODE #8

E: Okay, somebody told me . . . you said that you are planning to go there.

S1: Yes, I was reading about southern Spain, but I was looking to the map and there is a lot of sea there.

E: A lot of sea there?

S1: I don't know; I no go to Spain so much time. I think there are a lot of must see even aside the beaches and aside the sea.

E: In addition to going swimming in the ocean, there's a lot of things to see there.

Elizabeth's reflective comments (student motivation and involvement):

[A]One of the students, the student from Turkey, made the comment that there's really no reason to go there if you can't do those things and that comment had sort have gotten lost in the shuffle, so [B]I wanted to bring that up because it was a good point and I thought it could stimulate some further discussion among the students.

For Elizabeth, the more her students are actively involved in her lessons, the more opportunities they will have for language learning; thus student motivation and involvement are central to her reasoning. And while the class has jokingly concluded that based on this reading there is no reason to visit the Mediterranean coast, Elizabeth uses this opportunity (B) to stimulate further discussion and involvement among the students by asking (A) one student to elaborate on his plans to visit Spain.

At this point in the discussion, Elizabeth turns the floor over to two students who are from Turkey and asks them for their recommendations.

CLASSROOM EPISODE #9

E: How about our two guys from the Mediterranean, from Turkey . . . what would you recommend?

S1: Some parts of the Mediterranean are very good; there is no pollution. But some parts of . . . there's pollution. But, still, it's a very good place to see. And, also, you can see some part of our Mediterranean—it's possible. We have fishing.

S2: Also, a good place, Turkey is a good place if your purpose is not only just swim. There are a lot of history, a lot of historical remains. In fact, people usually call Turkey an open-air museum . . . open-air museum.

E: Open-air museum.

Elizabeth's reflective comments (student affective needs):

> [A]It's a chance for the students to use their expertise and to feel confident and comfortable about what they're saying and, whenever possible, [B]I like to give students an opportunity to share with the other students, but also to feel that they are experts about their own countries and experts in that knowledge, and they feel good about sharing that with the other students. So this is a chance for these two particular students to show what they know or to tell what they know and to inform the other students.

While many of Elizabeth's instructional decisions are made with consideration for student motivation and involvement, there are other times when she seems more concerned with the specific social and affective needs of her students. Elizabeth justifies this decision (A) in order to enable her students to feel confident expressing themselves in English. Yet she also wants them (B) to see themselves as experts and as having much to offer others, and to feel good about themselves.

Elizabeth dismisses the class by reminding the students to save this reading passage because they will be using it again on Friday. She reflects out loud about how much information they got from this reading without having to read the entire passage, emphasizing once again the value of scanning for specific information. Even though there is a fifteen-minute break between classes, most of the students remain in the room, listening with interest to the two students from Turkey as they continue to describe prime tourist spots along the Mediterranean coast.

Elizabeth's reflective comments:

> [A]This class was a nice mix. They got a chance to scan the reading and actually found out a lot about the Mediterranean coast without actually reading the entire passage. And they got to talk about things that they know about, like the two guys from Turkey. [B]I think it's really important for students to feel knowledgeable, to feel like they have something unique to offer the others. And this gave these two guys a chance to get into the conversation, into the discussion, and to give us some of their insights, provide us with some of their knowledge and get their point of view. So, it was good for the others too. We all laughed, but after scanning the reading they even said, "Why even go there if it's so polluted?' and these guys gave them some excellent reasons. [C]Overall, I think they were able to learn from one another and from the reading and they didn't have to read every word, or use their dictionaries.[D]They'll need to be able to do this to survive, so hopefully they realized this here.

Elizabeth describes the lesson (A) as a "nice mix," and this mix appears to consist of opportunities to practice an academic reading strategy as well as opportunities for students to feel knowledgeable and confident. Scanning will (D), Elizabeth believes, be an essential skill for students to cope with the demands of their university coursework. Yet she also believes (B) in the importance of making students feel knowledgeable and of their recognizing the value of learning from one another. She describes (C and D) this lesson as combining the competing demands of preparing students for the university and building their confidence in themselves as knowledgeable persons with much to offer and learn from one another.

Elizabeth's reflective comments illustrate that her reasoning is shaped by her knowledge of the skills and competencies her students will need to succeed outside her classroom, her knowledge of her students' unique language learning styles and strategies, her belief in the value of having students interact with one another in meaningful ways so as to learn from one another, and her desire to build up her students' confidence in themselves as learners and users of English. Elizabeth's reasoning is consistently shaped by her knowledge of two worlds: the world inside her ESL classroom and the world outside, in the university. For Elizabeth, it isn't knowledge that her university-bound students need, but rather the skills necessary to get at that knowledge, to make sense of that knowledge in a second language, and to take responsibility for their own learning. How Elizabeth manages the competing demands of the worlds inside and outside her ESL classroom is evident in the way she structures her classroom practices. In her final reflective comment, Elizabeth alludes to these two worlds and to how she tries to manage the competing demands embedded in each. It is the combination of these considerations that she believes will enable her students to succeed on their own, to take responsibility for their own learning, and to master the skills and competencies needed to succeed outside her ESL classroom.

1 REFLECTING ON REASONING TEACHING

The following Investigation asks you to reflect on Elizabeth's reasoning as a way for you to understand the complex nature of teachers' reasoning. It will also help you formulate a starting point from which you can begin to reflect on your own reasoning.

In your reflective journal or with other teachers:

A. What did you find to be the most striking feature of Elizabeth's teaching? Why? How is Elizabeth's teaching similar to or different from your teaching? If you were teaching this lesson, what would you have done differently? Why?

B. Reflect on Elizabeth's comments about her own teaching. Do you think about similar things while you are teaching? How are your and Elizabeth's interactive decision-making styles similar and/or different? Why do you think this is so?

C. Construct a concept map that visually depicts the complex nature of Elizabeth's reasoning. Include all the factors that seem to shape her pedagogical reasoning. How are they interconnected? What factors seem to figure more prominently than others? Speculate on why you think this is so.

Below are three sets of reflective comments that illustrate Ken, Anne, and Elizabeth making an instructional decision with consideration for student affective needs. Consider the following: How are these reflective comments similar? How are they different? To what do you attribute their similarities and differences? What does this suggest about the teachers' reasoning?

STUDENT AFFECTIVE NEEDS

Ken (classroom episode 6 see p. 85)

And I think it's important; a couple of the kids preferred not to take a guess, or not to take a chance. And there's really no winning or losing in this, and there's no, it's not, your name isn't going to be written up on the board if you guess wrong. A lot of these kids, and it may be with kids in general, but in this population in particular, really prefer not to take the chance. And, as a result, they either (a) don't get that satisfaction of being right, but (b) more importantly, they don't have to think it through. And that's really the core of what I'm trying to get at. So I always make sure, if the student says, "I don't really know, or I don't really want to guess," I say, "Well I'm going to come back to you, and then you can guess later because everybody's going to say what their idea is." And sometimes I have to wait it out a long time, but it's worth the wait, because the next time that particular student is more willing to give their answer. And after a little bit of practice, they usually come up with more accurate guesses than from their original "I don't want to try."

Anne (classroom episode 5 see p. 104)

Now he (S2) is new to the class, he is shy anyway, and now we have a video camera. But, I had to give him time. I try to give them all as much time as possible, not rush to the next person. But a way to save face for him was to kind of change the question, so that it's the same question, but someone else can now answer it for him.

Elizabeth (classroom episode 9 see p. 124)

It's a chance for the students to use their expertise and to feel confident and comfortable about what they're saying and, whenever possible, I like to give students an opportunity to share with the other students, but also to feel that they are experts about their own countries and experts in that knowledge, and they feel good about sharing that with the other students. So this is a chance for these two particular students to show what they know or to tell what they know and to inform the other students.

---

3 *Observing Other Teachers Teach*

Simply observing teachers teach does little to help us understand the reasoning and rationale behind teachers' instructional practices. However, when teachers explain their instructional practices, we begin to understand the wide range of

instructional considerations that influence what and how teachers think about their teaching.

Select an instructional consideration (Chapter 5, p. 58–59) that you wish to observe.

A. Observe a lesson and watch for the following:

- How does this teacher deal with this instructional consideration?

- How do his or her students respond?

- How successful is he or she at dealing with this instructional consideration?

- What might be some alternative ways of dealing with this instructional consideration?

B. Interview the teacher after the lesson and ask the following:

- How did you attempt to deal with this instructional consideration?

- How did your students respond?

- How successful do you think you were at dealing with this instructional consideration?

- If you taught this lesson again, what might you do differently?

---

4 CONDUCTING FORMAL EVALUATIONS OF YOUR TEACHING

Formal teaching evaluations are an important component of most professional development programs. While such evaluations can be intimidating, the more involved you become in the evaluation process, the more you will gain from the experience.

A. Set up a preobservation meeting with your supervisor to discuss your lesson. Give him or her a copy of your lesson plan and all relevant handouts. Be prepared to describe what you plan to teach, why you plan to teach it in this particular manner, and what you hope your students will be able to do as a result of the lesson.

B. Identify a particular aspect of your teaching that you would like your supervisor to observe. You might select a particular instructional consideration, a student you are having trouble with, alternative ways of presenting subject matter content, or ways of increasing student participation.

C. Set up a postobservation meeting with your supervisor to discuss your lesson. Before asking for your supervisor's feedback, describe what you believe were the strengths and weaknesses of the lesson.

D. Listen carefully to your supervisor's feedback. Try to summarize his or her major points in your own words (for example, "So what you are suggesting is that I . . ."). Request a written summary of your supervisor's comments.

E. Establish an Action Plan for Change to address your supervisor's concerns and/or suggestions (see Investigation 2 in Chapter 9, Creating an Action Plan for Change).

F. Set up a follow-up meeting or a subsequent observation with your supervisor to discuss your action plan for change.

9

TRACING THE DEVELOPMENT OF ROBUST REASONING

Throughout this book I have argued that the crux of learning to teach and understanding teaching lies in teachers' reasoning, defined as the complex ways in which teachers conceptualize, construct explanations for, and respond to what occurs both inside and outside their classrooms. I have argued that the robustness of teachers' reasoning resides in the completeness of their understandings of themselves, of their students, and of the classrooms and schools where they work; the flexibility with which they make use of these understandings; the complexity of their reasoning; and the range of instructional considerations they make use of as they teach.

Teachers who seek out opportunities to expand their understandings of the landscapes within which they work, who continually reflect on their own practices, and who critically assess the consequences of their teaching practices on their students' learning know what to do. They know what to do because they are able to assemble and apply what they know flexibly at different times, for different purposes, and in different situations. They know what to do because they know that in teaching it always depends, and they can articulate, to themselves and to others, the full range of considerations that it depends on.

Robust reasoning emerges within a lifelong process of engaging in critical reflection on and inquiry into teaching. To illustrate the different dimensions of this process, we return to Emily (Chapter 1) to trace the development of her reasoning after spending fifteen weeks teaching ESL freshman composition and as a full-time student in a master's in TESOL program. Then we will move to guiding questions that can enable teachers to continually engage in critical reflection on and inquiry into their own reasoning.

EMILY: KNOWING THE LANDSCAPE

It is now nearing the end of the fall semester. Emily has stopped by my office to ask if she can borrow my APA manual (*Publication Manual of the American Psychological Association*). One of her ESL freshman writing students located several sources for his research paper on the Internet and needs to be able to cite them correctly in the reference section of his paper. Emily isn't sure about how to cite Internet sources and neither am I. As I flip through my APA manual, I ask her what the student's research paper is about.

> **Emily:** He's really interested in professional sports and he started looking into professional basketball players' salaries and how they

are drafted and how they all have agents who represent them and that sort of stuff, and he found all this information on the World Wide Web . . . somehow he got into this discussion group where they've been talking about how young naive inner city kids are taken advantage of by the universities where they play basketball and then what happens to the few who actually make it into the NBA. He also found in this survey that they did that a really high percentage of inner city youth actually think they have a chance at making it to the NBA and only a tiny percentage ever do.

Karen: Sounds interesting.

Emily: And, you know, they have to do an interview for their papers and he somehow got in to see one of the assistant coaches on campus and he was all jazzed about it. I helped him prepare these questions and he was really nervous, but I guess it went really well and the whole class was so enthralled with his report.

Karen: Sounds like he really got into it.

Emily: I can't believe it because he's really into this topic, he's even come to my office hours a few times to talk about it, which is amazing because at the beginning of the semester he just slept through class. He wasn't a troublemaker or anything, he just didn't seem to care and now he's really into class. The other day he was telling his writing group about this on-line discussion group he got on and he was really into it, and they got really to it, and he was telling them about some of the crazy things people say in these discussion groups.

Karen: What do you think turned him around?

Emily: Well, he's really interested in this topic and I know at the beginning of the semester we were mostly writing about the readings in the book and they're pretty contrived, you know, lots of cross-cultural stuff. I mean the readings are good, and some of the students seem to relate to them, especially those who are new-comers to the U.S., but lots of these students have actually gone to American high schools, they're American, they think of themselves that way, they just don't speak English as their first language and most of them struggled in school because of this. They've had pretty bad experiences in school and especially with writing.

Karen: So you think letting him write about something he's interested in made the difference?

Emily: Yeah, for him for sure, but there were other students who couldn't think of anything to write about, and I'd say, "What are you interested in?" and they'd tell me and I'd say, "Write about that," and they'd give me these surprised looks, like they couldn't believe that it was OK to write about something they were interested in. I mean the whole purpose of this research paper is for them to learn how to research a topic, formulate an argument, take a position, and argue for it. The topic is really not all that important. I mean, they need to pick something that is researchable, but when they get in their upper-level courses their professors are going to assign a ten-page research paper and they are going to need to know where to start, how to find information, how to organize that information once they get it, and then the toughest thing is for them to say what they think about the topic.

Karen: Really?

Emily: Last week we had our first writing conferences and most of them had lots of information about their topics, but they just reported the information without any sort of interpretation on their part. I found myself asking over and over again, "So, what do you think about this?" It's almost like they don't realize that they can say what they think.

Karen: How are you encouraging them to do this?

Emily: Well, they're having to do several things.

Karen: Such as?

Emily: We've been working on summarizing, paraphrasing, and quoting all semester and now [for the research papers] they finally have a chance to really use them. Sandra [a TA who taught this course last year] told me about this great activity that she did that really got her students talking about what they thought, so last week I tried it and I had them bring in one article on their topic and they had to write a written summary and then give an oral summary to their writing groups. I told the group members to ask, "Given what you just told us, what do you think about this and why?" and I think this helped because they first summarized it and then they had to talk about it in terms of what they thought.

Karen: Were they able to do this?

Emily: Most of them. Sometimes I wonder if they've ever had the chance to say what they think about something. It's like they have no sense of the idea that what they think is important or that others might be interested in what they think. I guess that's just schooling in general: "spit back what the teacher tells you and don't think about it." But in writing you can't do that, you have to put your voice in it. I know this is tough to do, I still struggle with it when I write, but it's the key to good writing, I think.

Karen: How so?

Emily: Well, you have to be interested in what you are writing about, you have to care, you have to have something of yourself invested in it or it will be impossible to write. I had this history teacher in high school who made us write as if we were there. I remember writing this fictitious letter to my brother describing how I had just survived the bombing at Pearl Harbor . . . so to do this we had to find out about what it might have been like before the bombing, what our daily routine might have been, what we ate, what we did to kill time. It was really cool and I remember more about that time period in American history than just about anything else.

Karen: So by personalizing it, it became important to you, and your voice came through?

Emily: Exactly. And these guys don't get this. They think writing is about correcting grammar, not about ideas. They think if they just write it once and the grammar is correct then it's done. I know grammar is important, it needs to be grammatically correct. I know their professors won't tolerate grammar mistakes. But their ideas need to come first. They need to know what they want to say before worrying about grammar.

Karen: Have you convinced them yet?

Emily: Maybe some of them. We've been doing these self-editing profiles—you know, the ones in the support packet—where they keep a list of the kinds of errors they make most often in their writing and then they have to go through their own papers and look for these types of errors. This gets them to look for their own mistakes because once they leave my class, no one is going to help them with grammar. In fact, their professors will think they are dumb or lazy if they hand in papers with grammar mistakes. One of my students told me he went to the Writing Center on campus and they told him they don't deal with grammar. Can you image that? They don't deal with grammar! Isn't grammar how we express meaning? Didn't we learn that in your class?

Karen: Sure, but I suspect the Writing Center tutors either assume that grammatical accuracy is a prerequisite skill or they just have no idea how to help ESL students with grammatical problems. They have probably been told by their supervisors not to correct grammar.

Emily: But lots of Americans have problems with grammar too, it's not just an ESL thing. I keep telling my students that, but anyway these self-editing profiles seem to help them focus on just a few grammar problems at a time, the ones they make all the time.

Karen: Does it help?

Emily: Yes, for minor stuff like prepositions and articles, but for some of them it's more complicated than that, so we've also been doing reformulations. You know—where we write a sentence or paragraph several different ways and then talk about which way expresses the ideas of the author best. I'm still working on this. I can empathize with them—I remember what it was like to write in Spanish. I was always more worried about being grammatically correct, but that's what we got graded on, whether it was correct or not, not on the substance of what we were trying to say. So I understand where they are coming from, it's sort of like changing the whole idea of writing. And I think they're beginning to realize the value of multiple drafts. In the beginning, they wrote something and then handed it in. Now they'll say things to me, like "This is just a rough draft" or "I was just trying to get my ideas down on paper." So I think they now see writing as more of a process than a product. And I think some of them are actually learning something about themselves by going through this process.

Karen: It sounds like it's been a hard sell.

Emily: It has, but for some of them the idea of writing as a process is all new. In fact, we had this long discussion about plagiarism and why it's such a problem in American universities. Some of the students said they would be marked down if they put the words of some great writer into their own words. And they all felt that they couldn't express things better than most authors so they just use the author's words. Some of them didn't even know what plagiarism is or why it is viewed so negatively in academic circles.

Karen: Did you tell them it's a problem for American students too?

Emily: And I told them about the Harvard professor who was forced to resign because some of his publications were found to be plagiarized. They couldn't believe it. Sandra gave me some of her students' papers from last year that were plagiarized and I passed out copies and asked them to decide what was plagiarized and it was amazing how easily they were able to find them. And I warned them that it would be that easy for me when I read their research papers. So I think we're making progress. We'll see; the papers come in next week.

Karen: What are you expecting?

Emily: Well, I'm expecting the standard stuff—you know, they need a thesis, they have to support their position, they need to present both sides of the issue, it has to be organized and coherent and all that stuff, and grammatically correct. But what I want is to hear them in their papers. I want to know that they learned something new, that what they learned is important to them, that they care about some issue enough to argue for it, to build a case, to convince others, to say what they think and back it up. This is what I'm hoping for, and if they do this in my class, maybe they'll remember this experience and the next time they have to write a research paper they'll know what to do.

EDUCATIVE EXPERIENCES: TRACING THE DEVELOPMENT OF ROBUST REASONING

From this conversation I have the strong sense that Emily knows what to do. She knows what to do because she knows so much more about the landscape in which she works than she did at the beginning of the semester. Emily knows her students. She knows what her students are interested in and she knows they become more motivated and involved when they write about something they are interested in. She has some sense of what her students' previous schooling experiences were like (both within and outside the U.S.), knowing that most have had negative experiences as second language writers with few opportunities to express themselves in their own writing. She understands her students' conception of writing as correcting grammar and recognizes that this differs dramatically from her own conception of writing as a process within which writers construct meaning.

What Emily knows about her students is balanced against what she knows about herself as a writer and a teacher. She has a clear sense of what good writing is based on, beliefs that are grounded in her own experiences as a writer. She knows what sort of writing experiences made a difference for her and she wants her students to have such experiences too. She knows what it is like to write in a second language and can therefore empathize with her students' obsession with grammatical accuracy. Emily knows that she faces multiple and often competing demands as a teacher of writing. While her students need to master certain academic writing skills to succeed in their university courses, she also wants them to reconceptualize writing, to see writing as a means of coming to understand something new, of self-expression, and as a means of learning.

Emily also knows about the learning environment in which her students will be expected to function once they leave her ESL class. She knows that university professors regularly assign research papers but rarely offer the kind of support and direction that ESL students need to research and write such papers. She also knows that most professors expect their students to have mastered basic writing skills (grammatical accuracy and organizational coherence) and, therefore, refuse to "waste" their instructional time on such matters. She knows that the academic community expects research papers to follow certain discourse conventions (thesis, organization, coherence, and so forth), be grammatically accurate, and reflect students' own words (not plagiarized). Some of this she knows from her own firsthand experiences as a student and some she is only now becoming aware of as she participates in her new role as teacher in an American university.

Emily's knowledge of her students, of herself as a writer and teacher, and of the university learning environment help formulate her justifications for why she teaches the way she does. She asks her students to use self-editing profiles because she recognizes the importance of grammatical accuracy in written texts in a university setting. Yet at the same time, using the self-editing profiles puts grammatical accuracy in a position secondary to the expression of ideas. For Emily, the self-editing profiles enable her to deal with grammatical accuracy without sacrificing attention to the formulation of ideas or meaning-making that occurs through the process of writing. In addition, the self-editing profiles force her students to become editors of their own texts, something Emily recognizes as essential if her students are to be successful in their university courses.

Emily's knowledge of herself as a writer and her conception of good writing also serve as justifications for her instructional activities. As a writer, Emily recalls powerful memories of experiences that enabled her to find and use her own voice in her writing. She asks her students to present oral summaries to their writing groups so they will have opportunities to articulate what they think about the topics they are researching. She hopes this will give them opportunities to express their own opinions about what they are reading, which Emily sees as an important first step if they are to establish their own sense of voice in their writing.

As Emily talks about this class, she appears to weigh her knowledge differently, in different situations, for different purposes. Some of her instructional activities focus on mastering specific writing skills while others focus on developing students' sense of voice. Yet in the end, she hopes students' papers will not only conform to specified discourse conventions but also reflect what they have learned through the process of writing these research papers.

How Emily thinks about herself as a teacher and her teaching is shaped by her knowledge of herself as a writer, a learner, a second language writer, and a teacher. It is shaped by her knowledge of her students. It is shaped by her knowledge of the expectations of professors within an American university. It is shaped by the curriculum she is expected to teach and the skills and competencies her students are expected to master. It is shaped by her beliefs about writing and learning. For Emily, knowing what to do resides in her knowledge of the landscape in which she works. And teaching these students requires Emily to make use of her knowledge in flexible and interpretive ways.

At this point, you might ask if getting to know your landscape comes from simply spending time in that landscape, as Emily has for the past fifteen weeks. To a great extent, as we have seen throughout this book, teachers' knowledge is largely experiential. It is grounded in and continually reconstructed through teachers' real-life experiences both inside and outside the classroom. But it isn't just experience itself that has helped to broaden Emily's knowledge of her landscape. It's a combination of experience and deliberate reflection on and critical inquiry into that experience that has made Emily's experiences this semester, in

Dewey's terms, "educative" (1933, p. 46). That is, by participating in activities that promote deliberate reflection on and critical inquiry into herself as a teacher and her own teaching, Emily has begun to articulate, to herself and others, that every decision she makes, every alternative she considers, every action she carries out, and every interaction she participates in depends on a range of considerations that are endemic in both her and her teaching context. The "it depends" nature of Emily's reasoning becomes explicit as she constructs explanations for her classroom practices, which in turn enable her to understand those practices in light of all that she knows about the landscape in which she works.

For Emily, this has been a very intense semester. Besides teaching two sections of the ESL freshman composition course and taking three graduate-level courses as part of her master's in TESOL degree, she is also taking part in a rigorous TA training course. This course is designed to provide instructional support for TAs as they carry out their teaching duties, formulate weekly lesson plans, create appropriate instructional activities and materials, and develop accurate assessment measures to evaluate student achievement. The requirements of the course create structured opportunities for TAs to reflect on and learn about both themselves as teachers and their own teaching, to critically examine their own classroom practices and the classroom practices of others, and to work collaboratively with fellow TAs as they plan and carry out their teaching duties.

A semester-long requirement of the course is to keep a reflective journal (Investigations 1, Chapter 1). In addition, Emily attended weekly meetings with her fellow TAs in which they discussed and compared lesson plans and shared their concerns about issues that arose in their teaching assignments. Every few weeks, the TAs reflect on and discuss lessons that worked (Investigations 2, Chapter 6) and those that didn't (Investigations 3, Chapter 7). They each carried out two teaching observations, one of a TA teaching the current teaching assignment and another of a TA teaching the course they will teach during their second year in the program (Investigations 3, Chapter 8). In addition, each TA conducted an interview with a teacher (Investigations 4, Chapter 6). In Emily's case, she chose to interview a teacher in the local elementary school, since this is the context she expects to teach in once she graduates from the master's in TESOL program.

During the latter part of the semester, Emily's teaching was videotaped and she analyzed her instructional decision making (Investigations 1, Chapter 5), giving her an opportunity to articulate why she teaches the way she does and to make explicit the instructional considerations she thinks about as she teaches. In addition, on three separate occasions throughout the semester I observed Emily's teaching and after each observation (Investigations 4, Chapter 8) we met to discuss the lesson, I wrote a formal observation report, and Emily created an action plan for implementing change in her teaching (Investigations 2, Chapter 9).

To fulfill the requirements of her other graduate courses, Emily also wrote an autobiography (Investigations 4, Chapter 2) and read and retold stories about other teachers (Investigations 5, Chapter 2). She responded to and discussed with her classmates cases that illustrate certain instructional dilemmas (Investigations 4 and 5, Chapter 5), and she read, responded in writing, and discussed in class, an extensive reading list of research about teachers and teaching and second language writing.

By design, these activities foster critical reflection on and inquiry into who teachers are, what teaching is, and why teachers teach the way they do. They bring to the surface the justifications that teachers construct for their classroom practices, and they enable teachers to critically examine their justifications so that they can modify, alter, and/or transform those justifications as they see fit within the context within which they are teaching.

Thus, a combination of experience and reflecting on that experience has helped to broaden Emily's knowledge of the landscape where she works. Interestingly, however, according to Emily, her professional development experiences this semester entailed much more. At the end of the semester, I asked Emily to describe what she felt was the most worthwhile aspect of her first semester as a TA in our program. She immediately responded that it was "the informal stuff":

> We [fellow TAs] talk about our teaching all the time. If I have a
> bad lesson, I know I can go back to the office [desk-space in an
> open office area] and there will be somebody there I can talk to.
> Since we're all in this together, they know what I'm going through,
> chances are it happened to them too, and we'll talk about what they
> did, or how they handled it and somehow I end up feeling better. It's
> like if you can talk about it you can understand it better. . . . It's not
> that the other stuff [requirements of her courses] wasn't helpful—I
> know a lot more about myself now than I ever did before and I'm
> so much more aware of why I teach the way I do, . . . but having
> someone to talk to who knows exactly what you are going through
> makes a difference. When I was teaching overseas and even in my
> elementary school, I never really had other teachers I could talk to.
> Everyone did their own thing, nobody shared their stuff, it was like
> everyone was out for themselves, like if you told somebody about
> something you did, they'd steal it. But here, it's different. A couple
> of the second-year TAs taught my course last year and they're
> always giving me stuff or talking about what they did. They know
> what I'm going through because they went through it last year, so
> there is this openness between us that I've never had before and it
> makes a huge difference in how I think about my own teaching.

The importance that Emily placed on being part of a professional community reflects Britzman's (1991) notion that learning to teach is socially negotiated, not individually experienced, in that teachers' knowledge of teaching is constructed through experiences in and with members of their professional community. For Emily, "the informal stuff" took place within a community of teachers who shared common experiences, concerns, and needs. The combination of experience, reflection on and inquiry into that experience within a professional community created opportunities for Emily to engage in what Hatton and Smith call "dialogic reflection" (1995, p. 45). In other words, by talking about her teaching with others, Emily was able to analyze her own actions, construct justifications for those actions, and explore alternative ways to approach her classroom practices. Thus we can trace the development of Emily's reasoning thanks to the combination of these experiences over the course of fifteen weeks.

1 GUIDING QUESTIONS FOR THE DEVELOPMENT OF ROBUST REASONING

For teachers who are committed to the long-term development of robust reasoning, I ask that they consider the following guiding questions. These guiding questions are not intended to be answered in any particular order; nor should they be answered just once. Instead, I believe such questions benefit teachers most when they are pondered, explored, answered, shared with other teachers, reexamined, reexplored, and answered again and again throughout teachers' professional careers. By doing so, teachers remain lifelong students of teaching; they engage in deliberate reflection and critical inquiry into their own knowledge and practices; they are able to articulate why they teach the way they do; they are able to assess the consequences of their teaching practices; they are able to change their teaching as they see fit; and they continually expand their conceptual understandings of themselves, their students, their classrooms, and the schools where they work.

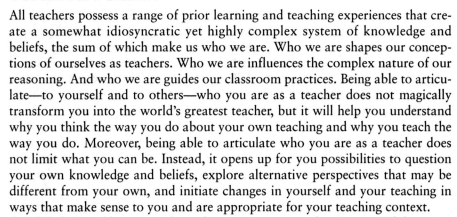

Guiding questions:

Who am I as a teacher?

Who are my students? How do they experience my teaching?

What do I know about my teaching context?

What do I know about the subject matter content that I teach?

Why do I teach the way I do?

What are the consequences of my teaching practices for my students?

How do I make sense of theoretical knowledge?

Who is my professional community?

What sort of change do I see as fit for my own teaching?

Who Am I as a Teacher?

All teachers possess a range of prior learning and teaching experiences that create a somewhat idiosyncratic yet highly complex system of knowledge and beliefs, the sum of which make us who we are. Who we are shapes our conceptions of ourselves as teachers. Who we are influences the complex nature of our reasoning. And who we are guides our classroom practices. Being able to articulate—to yourself and to others—who you are as a teacher does not magically transform you into the world's greatest teacher, but it will help you understand why you think the way you do about your own teaching and why you teach the way you do. Moreover, being able to articulate who you are as a teacher does not limit what you can be. Instead, it opens up for you possibilities to question your own knowledge and beliefs, explore alternative perspectives that may be different from your own, and initiate changes in yourself and your teaching in ways that make sense to you and are appropriate for your teaching context.

While being able to articulate who you are as a teacher is essential, knowing who other teachers are is equally important. The questions that teachers ask of themselves they should also ask of other teachers. What sorts of prior learning and teaching experiences have others teachers had? What is it about those experiences that has influenced them the most as teachers today? What do other teachers know and believe about students, learning, and teaching? Why do they think about their teaching in certain ways? Why do they teach the way they do? How are your experiences, knowledge, and beliefs similar to and different from those held by other teachers? When teachers engage in sustained reflection and dialogue with others about who they are as teachers throughout their professional careers, it enables them to make explicit the knowledge and beliefs that shape their conceptions of themselves as teachers, their reasoning, and their classroom practices.

Who are my students? How do they experience my teaching?

The assumptions you make about your students have a tremendous impact on the nature of your reasoning and the nature of your teaching practices. What you know about their likes and dislikes; their strengths and weaknesses; their expectations for themselves and for you; their ways of acting, interacting, and learning within your classroom all factor in to how you think about your teaching and why you teach the way you do. Knowing your students also entails knowing as much as you can about their lives outside your classroom.

Obviously, knowing your students takes time, but it also takes a certain mindset on the part of the teacher. Knowing who your students are requires that you focus less on what you are doing as a teacher and more on what your students are experiencing in your classroom. This means examining your teaching practices from the perspectives of your students: determining what creates difficulties for them, what challenges them, what helps them make connections between what they already know and what you are trying to teach them, what sparks their interest, what they see as the purpose of your instructional activities, and what they get out of participating in your instructional activities. Knowing who your students are and how they experience your teaching is central to the development of robust reasoning.

What do I know about my teaching context?

Almost every teacher highlighted in this book made instructional decisions based on the learning context that his or her students will be expected to function in once they leave their classrooms. Because the context within which teachers teach has such a powerful impact on teachers' reasoning, it is essential that you be aware of how your ESL/EFL program is positioned within your own teaching context. This requires that you know how the school/program administrators, other teachers, and parents view the ESL/EFL program, and where you see yourself and your students fitting into the overall school/program curriculum. It means knowing what the philosophy of your school/program is and how the ESL/EFL program is positioned in your institution. It means knowing how the ESL/EFL students are viewed by other school/program personnel and by the community within which the school/program is located. It means determining what your students will be expected to know and to do once they leave your classroom, and it means articulating to yourself, to your students, to their parents, and to other school personnel how you intend to equip your students with the skills, competencies, and knowledge they will need to succeed outside your classroom.

Knowing your teaching context also means knowing the politics of school life. It means knowing what the chain of command is within your school/program, who sets school and curricular policy for the ESL/EFL program, and who are the key players who can help you make changes within the ESL/EFL program. Moreover, it means knowing what you can do if you feel your ESL/EFL students are being treated unjustly, thus ensuring that they receive the services they need and deserve within your school/program.

What do I know about the subject matter content that I teach?

Reflect for a moment on the last lesson you taught. How did you present the subject matter content of that lesson to your students? Why did you present it in the way that you did? By emphasizing one aspect of the subject matter content, did you neglect another? What are some alternative ways in which you could have taught this subject matter content? Such questions are important for teachers to continually consider and reconsider because how teachers conceptualize their subject matter content, what they choose to teach, and how they teach it depend on who teachers are, who their students are, and what sorts of expectations are placed on both teachers and students within the school/programs in which they work. Such considerations figure prominently in teachers' reasoning and therefore should be continually reexamined throughout teachers' careers.

Why do I teach the way I do?

What sort of instructional considerations do you consider as you teach? How do you think about these instructional considerations within the context of your own classroom? Which instructional considerations figure more prominently in your reasoning? Why is this so? I hope your answer to these questions is "it depends." Knowing what to do in any classroom depends on a host of considerations, and teachers' knowledge about these considerations and how they recognize, interpret, and respond to them shapes the complex nature of their reasoning and their teaching practices. Articulating to yourself and others why you teach the way you do forces you to reflect on your classroom practices, construct justifications for your classroom practices, question the basis of your justifications, compare your justifications to those of other teachers and, in some cases, alter and/or transform your justifications and your teaching practices in ways that are appropriate within your teaching context.

Getting inside the heads of other teachers and recognizing the complexity of their reasoning can enable you to see alternative ways in which teachers make sense of what they do. The same questions that you ask yourself about your own teaching should be asked of other teachers. What sort of instructional considerations do other teachers consider as they teach? How do they think about these instructional considerations? Which instructional considerations figure more prominently in their reasoning? Why is this so? How are your instructional decisions similar to and different from those made by other teachers? Why? Again, such critical inquiry into teachers' classroom practices makes explicit the complex nature of teachers' reasoning.

What are the consequences of my teaching practices for my students?

Imagine that you are in the middle of a lively class discussion and suddenly a student makes a crude remark about another student and the entire class laughs. How do you respond? Why do you respond that way? What consequences does your response have for your students? for the student who made the remark? for the student who was laughed at? These sorts of questions are critical for you to consider because they force you not only to critically reflect on your own classroom practices but also to seriously consider the consequences that your actions have on your students.

Every judgment, decision, action, and interaction that teachers engage in as they teach has some sort of consequence on their students as learners and as people. As Lampert (1985) argues, many of the problems teachers face in their classrooms are endemic to classroom life and therefore are not solvable, but merely managed. How you choose to manage classroom dilemmas will have consequences for your students, and it is therefore essential that you recognize that your teaching takes place in a sociopolitical and cultural context with real-life consequences for your students' lives. Articulating these consequences is essential because it will inform your reasoning and your teaching practices.

How do I make sense of theoretical knowledge?

Despite commonly heard complaints that theory has little relevance for teachers' daily classroom practices, theoretical knowledge can transform teachers' knowledge and teachers' practice, but only if teachers have multiple and varied opportunities to make sense of theory within the familiar context of their own teaching and learning experiences. This means reflecting on how a particular theory may or may not be relevant to your own second language learning and/or teaching experiences. It means reflecting on the extent to which this theory is consistent with your beliefs about how second languages are learned and how they should be taught. It means situating this theory within actual classrooms and exploring how this theory shapes your understanding of the instructional dilemmas that teachers face in that context. It means considering the ways in which this theory might be enacted within your instructional activities and trying out alternative instructional activities that are consistent with this theory. When teachers have opportunities to make sense of theory in terms of themselves, their students, their classrooms, and the broader social contexts within which they work, then theory becomes relevant for practice because teachers make it their own, and it becomes part of how they conceptualize, construct explanations for, and respond to what occurs within their classrooms.

Who is my professional community?

The professional community within which teachers work has a powerful impact on teachers' reasoning and teaching practices. Like a subculture, the underlying values, norms, and expectations shared by the teachers and other professionals with whom you work will shape, in part, the way in which you understand and respond to the actions and interactions that go on around you. If you hear from other teachers that a particular student is a troublemaker, chances are you, too, will view this student as a troublemaker. If teachers in your school regularly exchange their best teaching ideas, chances are you will too. For Emily, the lack of collegiality among teachers in her previous places of employment was in sharp contrast to the openness of the TAs in the master's in TESOL program. Whether you are entering a new teaching context or looking for opportunities for professional growth within the context in which you already teach, consider the following questions: Who are the other teachers you come in contact with on a daily basis? What sorts of beliefs do they hold about students, learning, and teaching? How are their beliefs similar to and/or different from yours? What do they see as the role of the ESL/EFL program? What sorts of exchanges do you engage in? What does and does not get talked about? What do you learn about yourself and your teaching from participating in these exchanges? What sort of role do you play in your professional community? What role does your professional community play in your growth as a teacher?

What sort of change do I see as fit for my own teaching?

What brings about significant and worthwhile change in teaching practice? Richardson (1990) proposes that teachers be involved in making judgments about what change is significant and worthwhile and, more importantly, be in control of that change. However, their judgments should not be limited to their own personal experiences, but expanded to include the experiences of others and their knowledge of relevant research. Richardson concludes:

> The outcome of a discussion that considers both sources (practical knowledge and value premises held by other teachers and empirical premises derived from research) around a particular topic, such as the teaching of science or reading comprehension, could lead to a socially constructed sense of warranted practice that can guide significant and worthwhile change in teaching practice (p. 14).

Teachers change all the time; however, the extent to which that change is significant and worthwhile depends, I believe, on the robustness of teachers' reasoning. Critical reflection and inquiry into your own teaching can help you make explicit the complex nature of your reasoning; however, doing so does not necessarily lead to change in your teaching. Teachers are often aware of aspects of their teaching that they wish to change, but they are unable to do so due to a variety of factors. The process of change occurs when teachers articulate to themselves and others what they want to change and why, when they identify the factors that inhibit change, and when they develop strategies to implement change over time. Change that is significant and worthwhile comes from and is controlled by teachers, it occurs with consideration for both knowledge and beliefs, it is the result of deliberate reflection and critical inquiry, and it requires the weighing of alternative possibilities within specific teaching contexts.

---

2 *CREATING AN ACTION PLAN FOR CHANGE*

Teachers are often aware of aspects of their teaching that they wish to change, but they are unable to do so due to a variety of factors. Creating an Action Plan for Change is an excellent way to articulate what you want to change, to identify the factors that inhibit change, and to develop strategies to implement change over time.

A. Examine a recent videotape of your teaching and identify one aspect of it that you wish to change.

B. Individually, complete the following:

One aspect of my teaching I'd like to improve/change:

_____

_____

_____

_____

Then create a list of (as many as you can):

Factors that inhibit change	*Strategies for improvement/change*
1. _____	1. _____
2. _____	2. _____
3. _____	3. _____
4. _____	4. _____
5. _____	5. _____

C. Work with a group; rotate the above information to each member of the group. Ask teachers to make suggestions for alternative strategies for implementing improvement/change in your teaching.

D. Individually, complete the following:

Three strategies I will use during the next two weeks to implement this change:

1. _____

2. _____

3. _____

E. Meet and discuss the extent to which you were able to implement this change.

---

3 *DEVELOPING A TEACHING PORTFOLIO*

Whether you are searching for a job or graduating from a teacher eduction pro-gram, developing a teaching portfolio is an excellent opportunity for you to articulate your conceptions of teachers and teaching to yourself and to others.

Complete any of the following:

A. Write a one-page statement of your philosophy of teaching. Include the following:

■ How do you view yourself as a teacher?

■ How do you believe your students learn best?

- What do you try to accomplish with your students?

- What do you hope your students will be able to do once they leave your class?

B. Describe one of your most memorable teaching experiences. What was memorable about it and why? Describe how this experience represents your conceptions of teachers and teaching.

C. Describe an artifact or object that represents who you are as a teacher and how you view your teaching (for example, a Swiss army knife: as a teacher I use multiple tools in my teaching to enable my students to learn English and I want my students to leave my class with multiple tools that they can use to function successfully in English).

D. Select three instructional activities that you feel were effective. Include an example from different grade and/or proficiency levels if possible. State the instructional objectives, outline the instructional activities, and describe what you believe your students gained from this unit.

E. Construct a one-page summary of student feedback. Describe how this feedback represents your conceptions of teachers and teaching.

Suggested Readings

John Dewey's classic book *How we think: A restatement of the relation of reflective thinking to the educative process* (D.C. Heath, 1933) highlights the interrelationships between reflection, experience, and learning. Dewey's ideas remain remarkably relevent to the issues we face today in both general education and language teacher education. I also recommend Virginia Richardson's book, *A theory of teacher change and practice of staff development* (New York: Teachers College Press, 1994) for a critical look at what it takes to enable teachers to make significant and worthwhile change in their own teaching practices. For deeply moving stories about how teachers change the way they teach, I recommend, Judith Newman's *Finding our own ways* (Portsmouth, NH: Heinemann, 1989), Michael Rose's *Lives on the boundary* (New York: Viking, 1990), Andrew Gitlin's *Teachers' voices for school change* (New York: Teachers College Press, 1991) and Eleanor Duckworth's *Having wonderful ideas and other essays on teaching and learning* (New York: Teachers College Press, 1987).

References

Barnett, C. 1991. Building a case-based curriculum to enhance the pedagogical content knowledge of mathematics teachers. *Journal of Teacher Education* 42 (4): 263–272.

Berliner, D. C. 1986. In pursuit of expert pedagogue. *Educational Researcher* 15 (7): 5–13.

Britzman, D. 1991. *Practice makes practice: A critical study of learning to teach.* Albany, NY: State University of New York Press.

Buchmann, M. 1987. Teaching knowledge: The lights that teachers live by. *Oxford Review of Education* 13: 151–164.

Calderhead, J. 1981. A psychological approach to research on teachers' classroom decision making. *British Educational Research Journal* 7: 51–57.

Carter, K. 1990. Teachers' knowledge and learning to teach. In W. R. Houston (ed.), *Handbook of research on teacher education.* New York: Macmillan, 291–310.

Carter, K. 1992. Toward a cognitive conception of classroom management: A case of teacher comprehension. In J. Shulman (ed.), *Case methods in teacher education.* New York: Teachers College Press, 111–130.

Carter, K. 1994. The case against thinking like a teacher. *Journal of Teacher Education* 45 (3): 236–238.

Clark, C. M., and P. L. Peterson. 1986. Teachers' thought processes. In M. C. Wittrock (ed.), *Handbook of research on teaching.* NY: Macmillian, 255–296.

Connelly, F. M., and D. J. Clandinin. 1988. *Teachers as curriculum planners: Narratives of experience.* New York: Teachers College Press.

Dewey, J. 1933. *How we think: A restatement of the relation of reflective thinking to the educative process.* Boston: D.C. Heath.

Elbaz, F. 1983. *Teacher thinking: A study of practical knowledge.* London: Croon Helm.

Feiman-Nemser, S., and M. Buchmann. 1985. Pitfalls of experience in teacher preparation. *Teachers College Record* 87 (1): 53–65.

Fogarty, J. L., M. C. Wang, and R. Creek. 1983. A descriptive study of experienced and novice teachers' interactive thoughts and actions. *Journal of Educational Research* 77: 22–32.

Freeman, D. 1991. "To make the tacit explicit": Teacher education, emerging discourse, and conceptions of teaching. *Teaching and Teacher Education* 7 (5/6): 439–454.

Freeman, D. 1994. Knowing into doing: Teacher education and the problem of transfer. In D. C. Li, D. Mahoney, and J. C. Richards (eds.), *Exploring second language teacher development.* Hong Kong: City Polytechnic of Hong Kong, 1–20.

Freeman, D. 1996. Redefining the relationship between research and what teachers know. In K. M. Bailey and D. Nunan (eds.), *Voices form the language classroom.* New York: Cambridge University Press, 88–115.

Fuller, F. F. 1969. Concerns for teachers: A developmental conceptualization. *American Educational Research Journal* 6: 207–226.

Gee, J. P. 1988. Dracula, the Vampire Lestat, and TESOL. *TESOL Quarterly* 22: 201–225.

Goodman, J. 1988. Constucting a practical philosophy of teaching: A study of preservice teachers' professional perspectives. *Teaching and Teacher Education* 4 (2): 121–137.

Grossman, P. L. 1992. Why models matter: An alternative view on professional growth in teaching. *Review of Educational Research* 62 (2): 171–179.

Grossman, P. 1994. Teaching and learning with cases: Unanswered questions. In J. H. Shulman (ed.), *Case methods in teacher education*. New York: Teachers College Press, 227–240.

Hatton, N., and D. Smith. 1995. Reflection in teacher education: Towards definition and implementation. *Teaching and Teacher Education* 11 (1): 33–49.

Johnson, K. E. 1992. Learning to teach: Instructional actions and decisions of preservice ESL teachers. *TESOL Quarterly* 26 (3): 507–535.

Johnson, K. E. 1994. The emerging beliefs and instructional practices of preservice ESL teachers. *Teaching and Teacher Education* 10 (4): 439–452.

Johnson, K. E. 1996a. The vision vs. the reality: The tensions of the TESOL Practicum. In D. Freeman and J. C. Richards (eds.), *Teacher learning in language teaching*. New York: Cambridge University Press, 30–49.

Johnson, K. E. 1996b. Portfolio assessment in second langugae teacher education. *TESOL Journal* 6 (2): 11–14.

Johnson, K. E. 1996c. Cognitive apprenticeship in second language teacher education. In G. Sachs, M. Brock, and R. Lo (eds.), *Directions in second language teacher education*. City University of Hong Kong: Hong Kong, 23–36.

Johnson, K. E. 1998. *Teachers understanding teaching: Installation, navigation, and investigations*. Boston, MA: Heinle & Heinle.

Johnson, K. E. and G. F. Johnson. 1998. *Teachers understanding teaching. A multimedia hypertext tool*. Boston, MA: Heinle & Heinle.

Kagan, D. M. 1988. Teaching as clinical problem-solving: A critical examination of the analogy and its implications. *Review of Educational Research*, 58: 482–505.

Kagan, D. M. 1992. Professional growth among preservice and beginning teachers. *Review of Educational Research* 62 (2): 129–169.

Kennedy, M. M. 1991. An agenda for research on teacher learning. NCRTL Special Report. East Lansing, MI: Michigan State University.

Lampert, M. 1985. How do teachers manage to teach? Perspectives on problems in practice. *Harvard Educational Review* 55 (2): 178–194.

Lortie, D. 1975. *Schoolteacher: A sociological study*. Chicago: University of Chicago Press.

Lundeberg, M. A., and G. Scheurman. 1997. Looking twice means means seeing more: Developing pedagogical knowledge through case analysis. *Teaching and Teacher Education* 13 (8): 783–797.

Nespor, J. 1987. The role of beliefs in the practice of teaching. *Curriculum Studies* 19: 317–328.

Nisbett, R., and L. Ross. 1980. *Human inferences: Strategies and shortcomings of social judgment.* Englewood Cliffs, NJ: Prentice-Hall.

Packer, M. J., and P. H. Winne. 1995. The place of cognition in explanations of teaching: A dialog of interpretive and cognitive approaches. *Teaching and Teacher Education* 11 (1): 1–21.

Pajares, M. F. 1992. Teachers' beliefs and educational research: Cleaning up a messy construct. *Review of Educational Research* 62 (3): 307–332.

Prabhu, N. S. 1990. There is no best method—Why? *TESOL Quarterly* 24 (2): 161–176.

Richardson, V. 1990. Significant and worthwhile change in teaching practice. *Educational Researcher* 19 (7): 10–18.

Richert, A. 1987. Writing cases: A vehicle for inquiry into teaching process. In J. H. Shulman (ed.), *Case methods in teacher education.* New York: Teachers College Press, 155–174.

Rokeach, M. 1968. *Beliefs, attitudes, and values: A theory of organization and change.* San Francisco: Jossey-Bass.

Schon, D. 1983. *The reflective practitioner: How professionals think in action.* New York: Basic Books.

Schon, D. 1987. *Educating the reflective practitioner.* San Francisco: Jossey-Bass.

Shavelson, R. J. 1983. Review of research on teachers' pedagogical judgments, plans and decisions. *Elementary School Journal* 83: 392–413.

Shavelson, R. J., and P. Stern. 1981. Research on teachers' pedagogical thoughts, judgments, decisions, and behavior. *Review of Educational Research* 51: 455–498.

Shulman, J. H. (ed.). 1992. *Case methods in teacher education.* New York: Teachers College Press.

Shulman, L. S. 1986. Those who understand: Knowledge growth in teaching. *Educational Researcher* 15 (2): 4–14.

Spiro, R. J., W. P. Vispoel, J. G. Schmitz, A. Samarapungavan, and A. E. Boerger. 1987. Knowledge acquisition for application: Cognitive flexibility and transfer in complex content domains. In B. K. Britton and S. M. Glynn (eds.), *Executive Control Processes in Reading.* Hillsdale, NJ: Lawrence Erlbaum Associates, 177–199.

Spiro, R., P. J. Feltovich, M. J. Jacobson, and R. L. Coulson. 1991. Knowledge representation, content specification, and the development of skill in situation-specific knowledge assembly: Some constructivist issues as they relate to cognitive flexibility theory and hypertext. *Educational Technology,* September: 22–27.

Sykes, G., and T. Bird. 1992. Teacher education and the case idea. In Grant, G. (ed.), *Review of research in education* (vol.18). Washington, DC: American Educational Research Association, 457–521.

Ulichny, P. 1996. What's in a methodology? In D. Freeman and J. C. Richards (eds.), *Teacher learning in language teaching.* New York: Cambridge University Press, 78–196.

Whitehead, A. N. 1929. *The aims of education.* Cambridge, UK: Cambridge University Press.

Yinger, R. J. 1987. Learning the language of practice. *Curriculum Inquiry* 17 (3): 293–318.

CPSIA information can be obtained
at www.ICGtesting.com
Printed in the USA
FFOW02n1552170716
25936FF

9 780838 466902